Lockdown with God

Finding your secret place

Marivic Quiazon

Copyright © 2020 Marivic Quiazon

ISBN: 978-1-8381-993-1-9.

DEDICATION

This book is dedicated to all my fellow travellers who find it hard to shut the door.

Marivic Quiazon
P.O. Box 146
Manchester
M30 0XN
United Kingdom

PREFACE

Throughout my reading years, I must have accumulated thoughts and inspirations from the many books I have cherished and loved. God used many missionary biographies to help ignite a fire in my heart for mission work. This turned into a zeal for the cause of Christ that has dominated my entire life. To these books I owe many of the thoughts and quotes which helped me to continue in serving the Lord even through trials and sufferings.

In writing this little book, I must have expressed some of these thoughts and inspirations and I have given credit to those I can clearly remember as I mentioned them in the book.

I hope and pray that you as a reader and fellow sojourner will be able to take something out of this book. If there is only one thing you can take, I pray you take with you the one thing that will not be taken away. Only one thing is needful, as Jesus rightly said to Martha, I sincerely wish that like Mary, you will choose to sit at the feet of Jesus and determine to do so in your secret place every day of your life.

Marivic Quiazon
July 2020

CONTENTS

Retire from the world each day to some private spot. Stay in the secret place till the surrounding noises begin to fade out of your heart and a sense of God's presence envelops you. Deliberately tune out the unpleasant sounds and come out of your closet determined not to hear them.

A. W. Tozer

If I have great things to live for, I will need less things to live on....

INTRODUCTION

23rd March 2020. UK joined the rest of the world in lockdown because of the corona virus pandemic. Suddenly, life as we know it has changed overnight. The following day, the unusual silence along the streets and roads of Britain has brought some panics among many who were not prepared for the sudden change. There was panic buying everywhere. There were questions and not infrequent thoughts of when it will all end.

Lockdown has brought the world to a standstill. No shopping, no gatherings, no business as usual, no visiting of friends and relatives, no sports, no schools, no church and no work. People were all asked to stay at home. Lockdown has begun.

In the initial week of this lockdown, I was still going to work. As a theatre nurse working in Recovery Room, we were being trained to support Intensive Care Units in caring for Covid patients. We were all preparing for the worst. It was difficult to understand how we felt as nurses during this time. There was a mixture of fear and courage as we found ourselves having to face the disease head on while the rest of the world was asked to stay at home. But the Lord took me out of all these. For reasons I do not understand, I found myself in lockdown. Little did I know, it will be a different kind of lockdown.

I was going to be in lockdown with God!

1

A different kind of lockdown

Only after all the noise has spent itself do we begin to hear in the silence of our hearts, the voice of God.

A.W.Tozer

As a person, I am always very driven and a doer. I get things done. I love projects and I thrive in achieving goals with a reckless determination. I can focus my whole attention to one worthy endeavour, and I'll be running and will not stop until I reach the finish line.

But I also love solitude. I have always known that there is power in silence, in being alone with your Creator and hearing His voice in your heart. When I was a little girl, I used to spend my early mornings sat under a tree at our backyard. I have my bible, the pilgrims progress devotional, and my journal. I remember staying there for hours looking outside watching the distant Sierra Madre mountains lining the whole periphery of the outstretched field behind our house. I loved listening to the sound of the birds and the wind blowing in my face. Then I would read my Bible and my devotional, I pray and write poems and sometimes I would write to the Lord. I enjoyed those times of being alone with Him. Those were precious times. I have learned to love Him there and get to know Him deeper in that place. Somehow it has become a source of great strength and power to me after I embarked on my own journey in life. My journey took me to England more than nineteen years ago now. I have been through tough times but it is this secret place that I have tried to maintain all my life that is the "one thing" I would say that has kept me going, loving the Lord and staying in His will all the days of my life. It has grounded me and allowed me to walk with God. People can see me being so full of life, animated and active. I do a lot of stuff, appears busy most of the time, sometimes engrossed with so many demands in ministry and mission. Travelling around the world and meeting new people, working with partners in various countries and the list can go on and on. If you ask me how I could do all that, I will be very quick in answering you that I can't. It is not me. So where does the power come from? In the movie Chariots of Fire, Eric Liddel preached once out in the open air and he asked the same thing; where does the power come from? And he answered, concluding his sermon, "from within". That is what the secret place is all about. Knowing the power from within. Finding my secret place in this lockdown is an opportunity like no other. It seemed that everything has slowed down around me. When I go outside, there was not many cars passing by, and I can see only one or two people on the road. This forced me to go back in. What shall I do? There is no work, there are no projects, no speaking engagements and no mission trips. I suddenly felt lost. I have always practiced a disciplined prayer life and reading and memorising the Word of God has been part of my life. But this one is different. It was as if the Lord is wanting me for an extended period! I realised, I was in lockdown to stay longer in my secret place. To stay in spiritual lockdown with God for a time and it was amazing!

The Bible talks about a secret place. Jesus mentioned this about prayer. Matthew 6:6 said "But when you pray, go into your room, close the door and pray to your Father, who is unseen. Then your Father, who sees what is done in secret, will reward you."

Being in lockdown has many similarities to what the Lord has been asking us to do for us to find our secret place. During lockdown no unnecessary travels are allowed. This means travelling only to buy food and if a key worker, then to go to work. Nothing else. One exercise allowed per day. In some countries total lockdown was implemented so it was even more restrictive. Restrictions from our normal existence must be sought to seek God in our secret place. We must give up our normal routines to give pre-eminence to this "one thing" that is needful. Jesus mentioned this when He was teaching Martha who was busy about so many things. Luke 10:42 says "But one thing is needful: and Mary has chosen the good part, which shall not be taken away from her." In this story, we found Martha, the sister of Mary being so preoccupied about so many things she needed to do, that she missed the whole point of opening her home to Jesus. She was the one who opened her house to Jesus, but she missed the whole purpose of His visit. Mary, on the other hand sat at the Lord's feet and listened to what He said. Because of all the distractions, Martha was upset and worried about many things as Jesus has pointed out. Sometimes, all the cares of this world come pressing upon us. It wants our attention each day. But here, Jesus was teaching Martha how to deliberately remove these distractions and learn to pause or stop so she can know His presence.

Being in lockdown with God will demand adjustments to be

made either by God Himself or by us deliberately. We need to silence the noises from outside and determine in ourselves not to allow these to hinder our time with God.

We all lead busy lives. There comes a time when we need to pause and think about deeper things in life. Lockdown has brought us all to this. It made us reflect on life and contemplate because we had to stop everything. Lockdown with God can be brought about by major changes in our lives. Trials and afflictions can sometimes be used by God to get us into this lockdown with Him. It is a different kind of lockdown because we would want to stay in it! There will be no exit strategies needed. The goal is to keep us into having this lockdown with God to guide our lives in our daily walk with Him. This will be our source of strength and power. Our kind of secret place where God can teach us and commune with us each day.

This is finding your secret pace. A place where we can be in lockdown with the Lord to teach us how to regularly stop and reflect. We can learn of the meekness of His heart, the less hurried existence that He wants us to live by. To learn to be still, to know the peace that comes with silence as we hear the voice of God in our hearts.

We are the ambassadors of eternity in the courts of time and it is our business to permeate the courts of time with the atmosphere of eternity....

Rev. Duncan Campbell

2

Entering lockdown (with God)

God never hurries. There are no deadlines against which He must work. Only to know this is to quiet our spirits and relax our nerves.

A.W. Tozer

The restlessness that comes to us when we are weaned from what is familiar reveals our true nature. As humans, we are creatures of habit. We dwell in the comfort of daily familiarities. It becomes our home unconsciously. We retreat to it whenever we are distressed or unsure. We look for it when we are in a new environment. We cannot rest until we find ourselves within the confines of this "little home" we made for ourselves throughout our lives.

When lockdown came upon us without warning, it was difficult to make sense of the changes that came so fast.

Literally, the whole world has changed overnight. No more familiar routines. We were all forced to comply to the new normal. But lockdown has brought so many good things to the planet. Clear skies, better air quality, peace and quiet in many streets and more time with family and loved ones.

I consider spiritual lockdown as a necessary component of our walk with the Lord. There are many Biblical examples of lockdowns where men and women of God have been deliberately taken aside for a time by the Lord Himself. Sometimes, it was a conscious choice that someone who is truly seeking the Lord makes, to seek His face and find answers to pressing doubts and questions.

Entering lockdown with God can happen unexpectedly. Sometimes when we are left with nothing else, when we have exhausted all our human strength in trying to solve our problems or when we are up against the wall, we find ourselves entering lockdown with God. It is like being confronted by a Higher authority and you have got nowhere else to turn to. You have been cornered by the Lord.

We see ourselves entering spiritual lockdown when we have been at the lowest point of our lives. We turn to God as a desperate last resort only to find that He was what we were looking for along the way. God is gracious and very loving. He always watches our steps and take us back in the right path when we go astray. But when we became so complacent and rebellious, wanting our own way all the time, He steps in. That is when we enter a spiritual lockdown with Him. When all the familiar routines are gone, all the usual entertainments and pleasure that distract us from Him and even the necessary stuff like jobs and attachments with people we associate with are temporarily paused, we find ourselves alone with God. To be alone with the Lord is the classic feature of spiritual lockdown. Here, we are faced with a pressing and daunting realisation that our greatest need is Him. The ultimate longing of the heart is God Himself. To taste and see that the Lord is good is a personal experience of a man or woman who have encountered the Lord in a profound way... with their own eyes. Like when Isaiah saw the Lord in Isaiah chapter 6. He saw the Lord high and lifted up and He was forced to confront His own sinfulness after seeing the Lord's holiness and His terrain. His own eyes have seen the King and He was never the same.

When we enter this lockdown with God, we are entering an unfamiliar territory. We will not be in control. There will be rules and adjustment for us to hear His voice and encounter

Him in a deeper way. There will be lots of waiting upon the Lord. Remember when Elijah was wanting to find Him, the prophet took a while before He can know where the Lord was. He finally found Him when He heard a still small voice. I Kings 19:11-13 says, "Then He said, "Go out and stand in the mountain before the Lord." And behold the Lord passed by and a great and strong wind tore into the mountains and broke the rocks in pieces before the Lord, but the Lord was not in the wind; and after the wind an earthquake, but the Lord was not in the earthquake; and after an earthquake a fire, but the Lord was not in the fire; and after the fire a still small voice.

So it was, when Elijah heard it, that He wrapped his face in his mantle and went out and stood in the entrance of the cave. Suddenly, a voice came to him, and said, "what are you doing here, Elijah?

Surely this encounter with the Lord must have a dramatic impact in Elijah's life. Yet, it took a lot of waiting to find the Lord. He was found by him and it was in the silence where the prophet must have least expected to find the Lord in all His majesty and grandeur! It was a simple, still small voice. Sometimes when we determined to seek and find, our patience will be tested. But the Lord promised us that those who truly seek Him with all their heart shall find Him. Jeremiah 29:13 says, "You will seek me and find me when you search for me with all your heart."

Let us enter our spiritual lockdown with God wholeheartedly with a longing only He can fill. Let us come out of the lockdown determined to return again and again, because we have found our greatest treasure within this secret place.

3

How to find your secret place

Oh, let the place of secret prayer become to me the most beloved spot on earth.

Andrew Murray

But when you pray, go into your room, close the door and pray to your Father, who is unseen. Then your Father, who sees what is done in secret, will reward you. "

Matthew 6:6

Shut the door. Why did Jesus talk about shutting the door when we enter our room to pray? Did He mean a literal room? Why did He emphasise this kind of prayer as if it must be in secret? What reward was He talking about which the Heavenly Father will give to those who learned to shut their doors in prayer?

To shut the door when we enter our private room is to be alone inside and by closing the door behind us, we intend to not let anyone in. So, shutting the door does not necessarily mean to always pray inside our room but it means allowing ourselves to be alone with our Heavenly Father and this can be anywhere! You can be out in the woods as you do your morning walk or out in the field or in the middle of the forest or by the hillside. To shut the door is to be away from the world around us, people, work, pressing needs, ambitions, dreams. It is a call to be alone with God. Jesus himself went to pray alone. Sometimes in the garden by Himself, on a mountain He spent whole night in prayer alone with the Father. Sometimes he got up before dawn and pray alone. We need to be alone.

Why is such emphasis on being alone, in shutting the door from the outside world, from the noises of our daily existence? Because prayer requires that we reveal who we truly are before an all-knowing God. Prayer requires complete transparency, truth, not even a hint of pretension must be found in our hearts when we pray and this requires that no eyes can see us, no ears can hear us but God Himself. Only when we are alone with God can we truly be honest with ourselves. When alone with God, we have no one to impress, we do not need to be conscious about what others will think of us. When we enter this privacy with God and shut the door, we are opening our true self to the Lord with all our brokenness and frustrations, secret sins and burdens we cannot tell even our closest friend. You are alone with God. The world is not in your heart, it is far away. Its noises cannot be heard. You have put out your business, your work, your own dreams, and your pleasures aside. Alone with God. God is near you and you are alone with Him.

This principle of shutting the door is applied even to our ordinary life. We shut our doors when we want to be intimate and alone with someone we love. Because we do not want anyone to disturb us or distract us from this precious time with our beloved. Even among the best of friends, there is a communion when being alone together is the sweetest thing. These two souls come together and shut the door from the outside world. Then they can share their secrets in their aloneness. No other ears can hear, no eyes can see them. Their fellowship seems perfect.

But these human intimacies cannot be full and perfect. Why? Because for intimacy to be perfect, we need to be fully known by the other. Not even the closest person to us in this life can claim that they fully know us. We cannot say this of anyone, that we found someone who completely and perfectly know us. Even our closest companion, a husband or wife can never tell perfectly what is inside the depth of our hearts. Each of us is a world in itself, our life continues to expand, and no one can fully know us except God.

When you enter your secret place with God, which is a place where you can be alone with Him and was able to shut the door from everything in the world, no noise, no other voices linger in your ears, then you are in the presence of the One who knows you perfectly. Then after you have been with God alone you can come out from that closet with full assurance that you are fully known by your Father in heaven. This is the time when you have learned to truly pray.

How do you shut the door in the modern day we live in right now? The constant flow of information threatens the very possibility of us to ever be allowed solitude. Social media became engraved in the fabric of our everyday existence. The constant beeping sound demands our immediate attention as if we must attend to its every call. The reality is that we have been enslaved and addicted by the same technology that promises us a better life. This is the first one we need to deal with to help us to learn how to shut the door.

I know this will be hard. But the first step to finding your secret place is to learn to shut the door. This means to shut the world around you. To learn to be alone with God. To learn to silence all the noises from your ears. The world is hectic and will pull you to what it wants all the time. You will need to learn to undo and release the hold it has on you. How will you shut the door?

Fasting & Self control

First, you need to have self-control. Self-control is the promised fruit of the Holy Spirit in our lives, but it will need your cooperation. I found that the most effective way to practice this fruit and exercise its power is through fasting. Before you embark on this journey of finding your secret place, you must be sure to have this established in your soul. You will need self-control to shut the door. Fasting will greatly help you in dealing with self-control. Our most basic addiction is food. We eat even if we are not hungry because that is what we have learned to do over the years. Fasting will release you from this addiction and

20

will teach you to control any craving you have during the fast. It also helps us to focus and become sensitive to spiritual things. We become hungrier for spiritual food when we silence the voice of our body. You can start fasting gradually. First, try to fast for one meal a day. Then try a one day fast, then 3 days and as you are led, you can try longer fasts. At the time of writing this book, I am in lockdown. I am also in the middle of a 7 day fast. Fasting is a powerful spiritual discipline. It can help transform your christian walk. I believe it is very strongly associated with the power found in the secret place. After all, prayer and fasting go hand in hand. Once you learn to fast, your self-control will be strong. You can then have the power to shut the door.

Switch off your phone, iPad, laptops and any social media gadget

Let us start with social media, this includes smart phones, iPads, laptops. If you decide to shut the door, these should not come inside with you! They must be left outside at all cost! You will be surprised at how much hold these gadgets have on us. The peace that comes with being able to shut them down for a time is amazing. It is also quite empowering.

Studies have shown that the allure of social media lies in its ability to trigger the centre of addiction in the brain. Similar to alcohol or drug tolerance mechanism, social media gives us a certain high when we received likes on our posts and so we become addicted to posting new photos or anything that might get us similar reaction from social media friends. It is like a kind of approval addiction. Our brain thrives on new feeds until it craves it all the time. Have you ever noticed how many times people look at their phones unconsciously?

When there is no internet or Wi-Fi connection, some people specially teenagers feel panic, like withdrawal symptoms from drug addiction or alcohol dependence. If we misplaced or lost our phone, we become restless until our hands can feel it again. This has become the norm and quite frankly clearly show how dependent we have become to this technology.

If you want to find your secret place, this must be managed and controlled in a healthy way. We should not let our lives be ruled by these gadgets. We must learn to use it to our advantage instead. Sharing blessings and praise reports through social media can encourage others. Giving positive affirmations and exhortations can help some lonely souls out there struggling with depression. If used this way, technology can be a blessing. But if we let it steal our time and control us, then it can become a curse instead.

Attachments/ people/ loved ones must be outside the door

The next to stay outside is your attachments, your love ones, all the people around you. Remember the first and most important commandment is "Love the Lord your God with all your heart and with all your soul and with all your strength and with all your mind." (Luke 10:27)

Jesus shutting the door means leaving His disciples and the multitudes behind Him and going up on the mountain in the middle of the night to be alone with His Heavenly Father! If you are a mother with young children, how can you shut your door ?

It can be anywhere in the kitchen while you are doing your routines and the children are asleep! I find the kitchen an incredibly special place to talk to the Lord. When I do my morning juice, as I chopped all the greens and vegetables, I commune with my Heavenly Father, whilst I worship Him too. I can recall many powerful encounters with the Lord in my kitchen! There will be many ways to get away from it all. I use my morning runs to be alone with God every day. With the earphone in my ears, I listen to my favourite worship songs and praise Him along with the trees and birds in the park. It is one of my secret places. Let the Lord lead you in your search for your secret place. I can assure you that you will find it as you seek to know His presence in your life. The presence of God is in the secret place.

Dream Big and Limitless

Work/ambitions/dreams/pleasures must be left outside

Setting aside what sometimes define us is difficult. But there is no place for ambitions and earthly dreams in the secret place. If we are to find this secret place, we must learn to leave everything behind us. When Jesus called on to Peter and John, they were in the middle of fishing, their occupation. Not only that but they have just experienced a remarkable success in their endeavour. They had a big catch, more than what they can handle! But that's with the help of Jesus, He revealed himself to them through the miracle of that catch. They have been fishing all night, but they got nothing. The miracle they saw opened their eyes and they followed Jesus at short notice, leaving everything behind. This is what we will find in the secret place. The presence of God is a treasure beyond our wildest dream! Answers to all our problems and troubles in life are found in the presence of God.

Pray to your Father who is in secret (unseen)

Prayer in its very essence is communion with God. To be in communion with someone, there needs to be a sharing, an understanding of each other. One needs to be known by the other so that they can have a meaningful communion. In prayer God wants to be known as our Father. Jesus said, "Pray to your Father who is in secret". Of all that is revealed to us about the character of God and who He is, God being our Father is the name which we can all relate to and understand. 'God is my father' is the most comforting statement anyone can utter in this life. It embodies God as our provider. Being a father, He will provide for all our needs. When we enter our prayer closet and shut the door behind us, we are in the presence of the One who knows and understands our hearts completely. He knows who we are with all our weaknesses, our struggles, our dreams, and embarrassments. There is nothing we need to hide from the One who sees everything. This makes this time alone with God, this communion, the most important aspect of our Christian life. Here lies the secret of power in our walk with Him and in our daily witness to others around us. We must take heed and stop to find our secret place.

The secrecy in prayer that is taught here by Jesus has to do with our inner motivation. Looking at the context of Matthew chapter 6, we can see that Jesus was teaching against doing our good deeds to be seen by men. Man's approval was the paramount motivation when people are doing charity in Jesus days. It was a radical message. People were accustomed to showcase their acts of good will in front of people. Approval of men was sought by even the religious leaders at the time. In Matthew 6:1-4, we read; "Be careful not to practice your righteousness in front of others to be seen by them. If you do, you will have no reward from your father in heaven.

So, when you give to the needy, do not announce it with

trumpets, as the hypocrite do in the synagogues and on the streets, to be honoured by others. Truly I tell you, they have received their reward in full. But when you give to the needy, do not let your left hand know what your right hand is doing so that your giving maybe in secret. Then your Father, who sees what is done in secret, will reward you."

God looks at our hearts. He wants to find purity and sincerity in our prayers. He repeated what He said here about giving to the needy to when we pray to the Father in secret; " Then your Father, who sees what is done in secret, will reward you" It doesn't mean we should not pray in public. It only means that He is after the motives of our hearts in everything that we do. He said that a broken and contrite heart, He will not despise (Psalms 51:17). True sincerity and purity of motives are displayed in brokenness. With it, we have been stripped of our self-righteousness and the desire to appear whole and in control. When we are broken, we render ourselves vulnerable and no more self-consciousness covers us. It is just a broken and contrite heart where sincerity and purity are found. These are the people God noticed and He rewards them by revealing Himself to them and answering their deepest prayers. Rewards await those who will find their secret place and are willing to tarry long enough until God shows up. Sweet communion with the Father is a reward that sometimes our heart will no longer wish for anything else. Yet God delights to reward His faithful children. He is a rewarder of those who diligently seek Him (Hebrews 11:6).

...who when he had found one pearl of great price, went, and sold all that he had, and bought it...

Matthew 13: 46

4

Treasures in the secret place

The kingdom of heaven is like treasure hidden in a field. When a man found it, he hid it again, and then in his joy went and sold all he had and bought that field. Again, the kingdom of heaven is like a merchant looking for fine pearls, who when he had found one pearl of great price, went, and sold all that he had, and bought it.

Matthew13:44-46

All our lives we have been searching. Searching for something which money cannot buy. We unconsciously seek for a more lasting happiness. One which will stay with us and not taken away.

Why would Jesus mention a hidden treasure in this parable about the kingdom of heaven? Why is it hidden, kept in secret, hiding in the field, and found only by those who diligently seek it. Another comparison is that it is like a pearl of great price and both seekers in the story sold everything they had to possess it. It is as if they were looking for this one thing all their lives and when they finally found it, it ended their search. What is the kingdom of heaven? If it's likened to a sought-after secret treasure, then, this must be what all of us has been looking for. Our heart's longing boils down to this one thing.

Only one thing is needed. When Jesus was teaching Martha about why Mary has chosen the good portion when He came to their house to visit, He said that only one thing is needed. What is this one thing which Mary chose instead of being busy with serving along with her sister Martha? Jesus also said that this one thing which Mary found will not be taken away from her.

If we compare this story to the parable of the hidden treasure, it make sense to see that this one thing that is needful is the hidden treasure of the kingdom of Heaven, the pearl of great price which once found will end all search. This is something that will finally satisfy our souls.

Encountering Jesus Christ

Jesus said "I am the bread of life. Whoever comes to me will never go hungry, and whoever believes in me will never be thirsty." (John 6:35). Here, we see the key to finding the treasure in the secret place. It is Jesus Himself. Knowing Jesus is the greatest thing, the one thing that we need. For this, Paul himself declared; "Indeed, I count everything as loss because of the surpassing worth of knowing Christ Jesus my Lord. For his sake I have suffered the loss of all things and count them as rubbish, in order that I may gain Christ."(Philippians 3:8) This was exactly what the merchant did when he found the pearl of great price, he went and sold everything that he has in order to gain it.

Like the man who found a hidden treasure in the field, after hiding it again, he also went and sold everything he has to buy that field. These show us that when we finally find what we are looking for in Jesus, our soul will be satisfied, and it will stop the never-ending search for what truly satisfies. Augustine of Hippo once said; "Thou has made us for thyself, oh Lord, and our heart is restless until it finds its rest in thee."

When we enter our secret place, we are seeking the face of God, in Jesus, we see the Father, for Jesus came to reveal Him to us. In the person of Christ, we are getting to know the Heavenly Father. That is why when His disciples are asking Him to show them the Father, He replied telling them that they have already seen the Father by seeing Him! We see this account in John 14:8-9; "Philip said, "Lord, show us the Father and that will be enough for us. Jesus answered: Don't you know me, Philip, even after I have been among you for such a long time? Anyone who has seen me has seen the Father. How can you say, "Show us the Father"? Likewise, in this present time, the role of the Holy Spirit in the secret place is indispensable. John 16:13-14 "But when He, the Spirit of truth, comes, He will guide you into all truth. He will not speak on His own; He will speak only what He hears, and He will tell you what is yet to come. He will glorify me because it is from me that He will receive what He will make known to you." Similarly, in John 12:49; Jesus said; "For I did not speak on my own, but the Father who sent me commanded me to say all that I have spoken." The mystery of the trinity.... our triune God whom we are meeting in the secret place cannot be compared to anything on this earth. It is indeed a treasure beyond compare. The treasure of all treasures.

The knowledge of God and His ways

Hosea 6:6 says, "For I desire steadfast love and not sacrifice, the knowledge of God rather than burnt offerings." In the

New Living Translation, the last part says; "I want you to know me more than I want burnt offerings." The Lord desire that His people know Him. At the time of Jesus, He emphasised the same thing. In Matthew 15:8; Jesus said, "These people honour me with their lips, but their hearts are far from me." He was addressing the descendants of the same people whom the Lord was talking about at the time of the prophet Hosea. They only offer sacrifices, but their heart is not in it. They were doing it as a duty or because it was the tradition in their society. There was no personal knowledge of the living God. One can be attending at the church regularly and even serving in the ministry but not know the Lord. You can even read your Bible but not know the God of the bible personally. You have not encountered Him, His reality. Your own eyes must see the King, like when the prophet Isaiah saw Him. It is possible to lose God in the wonders of His word. We can sing great worship songs but without the knowledge of God, it means nothing. The verses of the songs become real only once you have tasted and seen the Lord with your own eyes. This is what we will discover in the secret place. One of the treasures in this secret place is the intimacy with God that is being offered to those who will seek His face with all their hearts. He will teach us His ways. He will give us an understanding of who He is. This is what the Holy Spirit is doing in our hearts every time we checked in to the secret place. He reveals Jesus to us. We are having the knowledge of God. This is the treasure we find in the secret place.

Acquaintance with the Holy Spirit

When we come to the secret place, we are building a deep acquaintance and relationship with the Holy Spirit. We will learn to discern His voice. Acquaintance with the Holy Spirit will help us know the will of God in every area of our lives. Our walk with God will we be more real and easier. Jesus said "Come to me all you who are weary and burdened, and I will give you rest. Take my yoke upon you and learn from me, for I am gentle and humble in heart, and you will find rest for your souls. For my yoke is easy and my burden is light". (Matthew 11:28-30)

As we get accustomed to this secret place, Jesus will become more real to us, He will be an abiding presence. This is what the Holy Spirit does. He makes Jesus known to us. He will be there in our secret place teaching us, helping us to pray, comforting us, strengthening us. In John 16:7, Jesus described the role of the Holy Spirit, He said; "However, I am telling you nothing but the truth when I say it is profitable (good, expedient, advantageous) for you that I go away. Because if I do not go away, the Comforter (Counsellor, Helper, Advocate, Intercessor, Strengthener, Standby) will not come to you (into close fellowship with you); but If I go away I will send Him to you (to be in close fellowship with you)." (Amplified)

The one important work of the Holy Spirit inside us is that He teaches us and reveals to us the truth. He makes the written word of God alive and powerful. Jesus said in John 14:26; "But the Helper, the Holy Spirit whom the Father will send in my name, He will teach you all things, and bring to your remembrance all that I said to you."

In the secret place, answers are found. Because the presence of God is in the secret place. The deepest longing of our hearts that transcends even the farthest stars can be satisfied in His presence. This is where we drink the living water, partake the Bread of life which Jesus Himself promised to give us. He said that whoever eats this Bread will never be hungry. Our satisfaction in this life is found in Jesus Christ, the lover of our souls.

John 15 also talks about abiding in the vine. This is a deep teaching about learning to stay in the secret place to abide in Him. Jesus said, "Remain in me (abide), as I also remain in you (through the Holy Spirit). No branch can bear fruit by itself; it must remain in the vine. Neither can you bear fruit unless you remain in me." (John 15:4)

The fruit of the Holy Spirit in our lives shows the extent of our prayer life, in the secret place, where He teaches us and purges us of the world's dirt. As we are still in the world, we needed a constant cleansing, this is sanctification and it is a daily process, part of our walk with God. Galatians 5:22-23 says, "But the fruit of the Spirit is love, joy, peace, forbearance, kindness, goodness, faithfulness, gentleness and self-control." The most compelling proof of the fullness of the Holy Spirit in the life of someone is living a holy life, separate, set apart from the world. The Lord has admonished us to love not the world neither the things that are in the world. If any man loves the world, the love of the Father is not in him. For all that is in the world, the lust of the flesh, the lust of the eyes and the pride of life is not of the father but is of the world. The world pass away and its desires, but whoever does the will of God lives forever. (I John 2:15-17)

Being set apart means we are separated from the world. This was the expected characteristic of every Christian. The early Christians know this, and they have lived a persecuted life. 2 Timothy 3:12 says; "Indeed, all who desire to live a godly life in Christ Jesus will be persecuted." The world will hate those who do not belong. This world is never our home, we are sojourners, we look forward to an eternal city, which is our real home, same way as Abraham and all our biblical ancestors. The problem with us is that we started to be so comfortable living in this world. We forgot we are citizens of heaven; we belong in another world. We are not living in light of eternity ahead of us. J. I Packer puts it well:

For today, by and large, Christians no longer live for heaven, and therefore no longer understand, let alone practise, detachment from the world...Does the world around us seek profit, pleasure, and privilege? So, do we. We have no readiness or strength to renounce these objectives, for we have recast Christianity into a mould that stresses happiness above holiness, blessings here above blessings hereafter, health and wealth as God's best gifts, and death, especially early death, not as thank worthy deliverance from the miseries of a sinful world, but as the supreme disaster... Is our Christianity out of shape? Yes, it is, and the basic reason is that we have lost the New Testament's two world perspective that views the next life as more important than this one and understands life here as essentially preparation and training for life hereafter.

Our generation of Christians in the west nowadays know nothing about persecution. And yet, we know that thousands of our brothers and sisters in other parts of the world are enduring so much suffering for the name of Christ because of persecution. However, here in the west, if only we will determine to live out our christian life as expected of us, godly and holy lives, standing for truth and justice, then we will definitely be looked upon as idiots or fools. We will be laughed at whenever we share the Gospel with passion. It is the least form of persecution we can suffer but we still will not want to have it. We have been silenced and we think it is okay because that is what society demands. We forgot our first calling and commission to go and preach the gospel to every creature. We forgot that we ought to obey God rather than men.

This however can be dealt with in the secret place. The more we know the Lord, the more we get to love Him. The more we love Him, the more we want to talk about Him. We can't help it. If you have been in the secret place, you will know Him deeper and you will know His abiding presence. This will make you live a holy life every day. This is where the passion comes from. It is like an altar you built for the Lord, where His fire comes each time you commune with Him. It's like a secret garden where God comes to talk to you in the cool of the day. No one comes out of the secret place cold and indifferent to their Lord and Saviour. This is a place where He can transform you into a courageous and passionate disciple.

These treasures in the secret place are worth more than your own life. Ones found, you will be happy to sell everything you have to possess them and to keep them for all eternity. And, yes, you will indeed keep them forever as Jesus Himself said talking about this "one thing" which Mary chose; that it will not be taken away from her.

... a time to tear and a time to sew; a time to be silent and a time to speak; a time to love and a time to hate; a time for war and a time for peace.

Ecclesiastes 3: 7- 8

5

The role of Silence

We need to find God. *And He cannot be found in noise*
and restlessness. God is the friend of silence. See how
nature- trees, flowers, grass grow in silence. See the stars,
the moon, and the stars, how they move in silence. We need
silence to be able to touch souls.

Mother Theresa

Silence. It's an unknown phenomenon in our
modern world. We have been accustomed to having noises
around us round the clock. The media bombards us with
constant flow of information and updates on just about
anything. Social media and its accessibility made our life a
never-ending chatter. It is hard to find a place where there is
complete silence in our modern existence. Yet, it is possible
to find silence within our soul.

Silence is defined as the complete absence of sound. It generally means absence of any kind of noise.

What is the role of silence in the secret place? Why do we need to learn to wait until all the noises from outside have all disappeared?

When we are alone with God, we learn to wait upon Him in silence and reverence. We patiently seek His face and wait to hear His voice. With an open Bible and silent prayer, the Holy Spirit will speak to our hearts and open up the word of God like a clear sky. We will hear from the Lord in the silence of our hearts.

The role of silence is very important in the secret place. It teaches us to reverence Him. It helps us to discern His presence and know His voice. When the noises from the world fell one by one, we will be able to notice the difference it makes in our ability to hear God. In silence, the Lord speaks.

Silence does not only mean the absence of sound in a literal sense but, spiritually, it also means the absence of clutters in our minds and hearts. Unspoken worries and pressing needs that concern us each day must be silenced too. It must be laid down before the altar as the Lord has told us to cast all our cares upon Him for He cares for us. (I Peter 5:17)

It is only in learning to be still, that we will know that He is God. Psalms 46:10 says, "Be still and know that I am God." What does it mean to be still? If you see the stillness of a lake you will understand that serenity of heart means almost like a surrender, a wilful submission to the will of God. To be still is to not try to say anything, or move or do something, it's like putting ones hands up when police wants to arrest you. It's a picture of surrender. Recognising that you are helpless and not in control. This is what being still means. Only when we come to this place that the Lord said, we will know that He is truly God. Why does God need us to be still before He can reveal Himself to us? It is because for as long as we fight against His will and if we think we are able to do it on our own, we will never see our desperate need for God's intervention. This is a recurring theme in many Old Testament's stories. Men and women who tried to exhaust their energies first, tried everything themselves before they run to the Lord in surrender.

Silence allows us to meditate on the word of God more powerfully. There is power in silence. It teaches us to look deeper into our souls. It helps us to focus on our praying. It teaches us to be sensitive to the voice of the Holy Spirit.

It is nowadays exceedingly difficult to find a place with complete silence. Where no distraction can enter, and sound is absent. The society we live in does not promote silence. And yet, even medically speaking, silence has many benefits to the human body. According to some research, silence lowers our blood pressure, boost our immune system, and benefits the brain chemistry by growing new cells! It also helps decrease stress by lowering cortisol levels and adrenaline.

Jesus spent many silent, lonely moments up in the mountain to meet with His Heavenly Father. They say that up in the mountain, during pure silence, there is this sound, people call it the sound of the mountain or the voice of God. It can only be heard in this utter silence. Up in the mountain, all the noise pollution and sound interference disappear. There in the silence of the night or the beginning of dawn, Jesus would oftentimes commune with His Heavenly Father before starting His work. Before He chose His 12 disciples, He also spent a night in prayer up in the mountain. (Luke 6:12)

Jesus chose lonely, deserted places to pray. He went to the garden to pray but many times He will pray at night or at dawn, times when people are still sleeping and there is still no noise around. The role of silence has been emphasised in many of the examples He gave us about prayer.

During this lockdown, I had many opportunities to spend my time in silence. It has been very healing and refreshing. I wrote a poem about my experience which I thought best to share here:

Be still my soul, the Lord has said. Be still and know that He is God.

There is a silence within my soul. It aches when disturbed by so much noise from outside. Pain and loss mingle with my longing soul.

I need to find this silence within my soul. Where only the voice of God can stay. Deep inside my heart this stillness lies unchallenged by His perfect will. It thrives with peace and joy. The world will never know.

I long to find this silence. This stillness within my soul. To hear His voice, to know His will deep within my heart.

Be still and know that I am God...
Psalms 46:10

6

Be still and know....

Be still and know that I am God. I will be exalted among the nations. I will be exalted in the earth.

Psalms 46:10

To be still is to know that He is God.

There are times when it is incredibly challenging to be still. We have the tendency to want to do something all the time. It is human nature to rely on our own strength and abilities. In the whole chapter 46 of this Psalms, we can see how the whole earth trembles and falls. All the scenarios of men losing its fortress and confidence on this earth were mentioned. The psalmist here is declaring that God is our only refuge.

"God is our refuge and strength, an ever-present help in trouble. Therefore, we will not fear, though the earth gives

way and the mountains fall into the heart of the sea, though it's waters roar and foam and the mountains quake with their surging." (Psalms 46:1-3)

We see here how the emphasis is to know who God is, how He is over the whole earth and how for that reason we must learn to be still, to surrender, in order to know and understand that He is indeed God, the Lord of all the earth.

When we come to our secret place, we are meeting an awesome God. He is to be reverenced and feared. He is also a God of love and justice at the same time. There is more to being still than what we are able to comprehend. When we are confronted by a Holy God who knows us through and through, there are no words to describe this meeting. The only option for us is to be still before His presence. Only when we are still and surrendered can we fully know the Lord. To be still before Him is to be able to hear His voice and see His face. When we are actively seeking the Lord, it teaches us to be still, to discover quietness and peace inside our hearts.

There is also a lot of waiting upon Him in silence. This is not easy for our flesh to do. Our flesh wants to take charge and take part. To be busy and occupied. But our spirit is willing to wait. It has the strength to endure the length of time involved in seeking the Lord.

Our spirit is eternal. It has no concept of time which our flesh has been accustomed to operating. Hence our flesh is weak and cannot stand to be still. It will require the strength of our spirit to overcome this if we want to know the Lord deeper.

The call to be still before the Lord is not a request but a command. It demands that we stop everything we are doing and focus on His presence. It demands that we quieten the noises inside our hearts and minds, the cares, the worries, doubts, and pride that will hinder us from hearing His voice when He speaks. It demands that we surrender our own plans, ideas, and human abilities. It demands that we submit to the One who knows us perfectly. It demands complete humility from us in acknowledging that there is nothing we can do, that we are nothing before a mighty living God. It requires that we stay still, silent, and reverently waiting. The psalmist said that in the presence of God there is fullness of joy. (Psalms 16:11)

This heavenly joy is perfect and not wanting or needing any top up, for it is full. The joy that the Lord gives us cannot be understood by the world, Jesus said, the world cannot give us this kind of joy. As we learn to be still before the Lord, we will know Him, His thoughts, His ways. We will know of the deeper things of God. Things that belong to eternity, where God is.

It is indeed a privilege to be invited to come to the presence of God, to come up higher into the throne room and know intimacy with God that was once reserved only to chosen saints. Now, because of the blood of Jesus, His death on the cross for our sins, this amazing grace is available to all of us, inviting us to come boldly into the very throne of God and receive help in time of need. (Hebrews 4:16)

This daily surrender is an important aspect of our secret place. Being still before the Lord in complete surrender of our hearts, our will submitting to His will is paramount to know that the Lord is indeed our Lord. It will allow us to see His ways, understand His will and know His plans and purposes. This is getting to know God in a deeper way. Suddenly, prayer now becomes a fellowship of the heart, rather than just asking for things. Prayer in the secret place is truly the seeking of God's kingdom first and His righteousness. When we learn this, we will understand why Jesus said in Matthew 6:33; "Seek first the kingdom of God and His righteousness and all these things shall be added unto you." "These things" represent the concerns of our hearts, daily needs and worries that we have, but we chose to leave these behind when we shut the door of our closet to pray and seek God's face. As we know Him, He deals with all these things and add them to us according to His will. If we learn to be still before Him, He delights to reveal Himself to us. We will then really know that He is God.

a life that reflects Christ
and a life that inspires faith

To be a worshipper that love God
then a co-worker with God

Oh to live for you for my
loving God is Everything

Purify the flame with every leaves
that awaken my will to
Show me the life to live,
want to know who I want to
Lord Jesus Christ
I will do what you want me
to do what you want me around

7

That I may know Him

That I may know Him and the power of His resurrection, and the fellowship of His sufferings, being made conformable unto His death.

> *Philippians   3:10*

Here was a man who has reached the summit of any spiritual ambition in his lifetime. By far, Paul, the apostle must be the greatest apostle of his time. He has founded churches in Asia Minor which became the foundation of the early Christian's walk with God. He embarked on treacherous missionary journeys and trained likeminded teachers and pastors to lead these churches. He has been in prison many times, beaten and tortured for the sake of Christ and the Gospel and yet remained unmoved in His faith. He is one of the most respected apostles in Christianity. And yet towards the end of his life, he said that his one ambition is to know Christ. This man has spent three years in Arabia to learn of Christ personally. (Galatians 1:15-18)

For Paul, accomplishments in Christian ministry cannot be compared to a personal knowledge of Christ. He wants to know Him more. He wants to understand Him deeper. He said he wants to know the fellowship of his sufferings and even become like Him in His death. This was a man who has already suffered so much as a follower of Christ. And yet he felt those were not enough. He wanted to know Him more.

I have just finished the book, "Tortured for Christ" by Richard and Sabina Wurmbrand. This moving book chronicled the life of this couple under the iron grip of the Soviet Union in Romania. Under communism and actively persecuting the christian church, the couple suffered tremendous amount of pain and loss, beaten, and tortured and many times left as dead. But they have emerged joyous and victorious out of this ordeal. They testified of this fellowship in the suffering of Christ that makes us know Him deeper. The joy that this brings cannot be compared to anything on this earth. Similarly, knowing many North Korean Christians myself helped me to view sufferings experienced by Christians in a different way. Surely the Lord use them to help us know Him in depth. It is not really the knowledge so much as the experience of His fellowship while we go through the trials of fire.

When we learn to enter the secret place, there will be a desire that will be born from inside our heart. A desire to know Him more and more. A longing for His presence, a hunger for His words like we have never had before. To know Him will become our priority each day. This is what the Psalmist is talking about when he said, "Oh taste and see that the Lord is good." (Psalms 34:8)

To know Him is to taste and see with your own eyes that the Lord is good to you personally. This is beyond you hearing the stories of other people about God's goodness in their lives. This is your own story. Your own experience of God. God wants to be known by you. In Hosea 6:6; He wish that His people know Him. The word "know" here means intimate knowledge. The kind of knowing between a husband and a wife. The Lord wants to reveal Himself to us in a deeper way. But He can be known only by those who truly seek Him with all their hearts. He promised to be found by those who seek Him wholeheartedly. You want to know the God of the Bible. Sometimes it is quite easy to lose God in the wonders of His Word. God is a person. The truth is a person. Jesus said, "I am the way, the truth and the life." We do not deal with doctrines or dogma in Christianity. We need to encounter a true and living God whom the Bible talks about. It is not just teachings and traditions but a living experience of God in each of our lives. That is what Christianity is all about.

Becoming like Him in His death

This is not martyrdom, but a desire to die to self-daily like what Christ did. To know Christ fully is to become like Him in His death. To learn to die to self, to the control of the flesh and each day, choosing to live for Him. This is knowing the power of His resurrection. When we die to self, we are alive unto God. So, we put to death the deeds of the flesh. (Romans 8:13)

To know Christ is our one magnificent ambition in this life. What a privilege it is to be given the chance to be acquainted with Christ in this life. Every day, when we checked in to our secret place, we are being given a wonderful invitation to come up higher into the very throne room of God and know Him deeper. The presence of God is the most healing presence one can ever know. In His right hand there are pleasures forever more, the psalmist says. (Psalms 16:11)

In this world, people pursue fleeting pleasures that can only give transient happiness, never lasting joy. But in the presence of God and in the knowledge of Him, we will know of these joy and pleasures that the world has never known. To know the Lord is to know these unlimited resources in the heavens available to us. This was what Adam and Eve knew in the garden of Eden. They have no need for anything for they were in the presence of God every day. They have no doubts, no questions, no unfulfilled longings, and desires because they found all the answers in the presence of God. In His presence there is fullness of joy! This was what we lost when we sinned against God. The joy that the knowledge of God brings was lost because of sin. We have lost our way but through Jesus Christ and His death on the cross, the shedding of His precious blood, now there is remission for our sins, we can return to the Lord and know His presence again. This is the ultimate purpose of the cross. To bring us all back in God's presence. To open the floodgates of heaven again and give us the knowledge of God and His ways so we can live for Him in this life. Surely, this is our greatest calling. This is worth living for and if needs be, worth dying for.

Guard your

secret place...

8

Guarding your secret place

Of all things, guard against neglecting God in the secret place of prayer.

William Wilberforce

In Greek Mythology, there was a famous story about the Achilles heel. He was undefeated in battles until his enemy found out his secret. It turned out, his only weakness was his heel. As the story went, after Achilles was born, his mother wanted to protect him from harm. So, she dipped him into the river Styx, holding him by the heel. In Greek Mythology, the river Styx had special powers. So, Achilles became invulnerable everywhere but at his heel. His heel was not covered by the water. He was later killed by the Trojan prince Paris outside the gates of Troy who shot him in the heel with an arrow.

Our praying in secret is the key to a victorious christian life. As a child of God, we are in warfare every day. We needed the protection of the power of prayer which covers us from any attacks from the enemy.

Why do we need to guard our secret place?

Because it is very easy to neglect this important area of our lives. We all lead busy lives and demands of our everyday existence can be overwhelming. We are to be vigilant in guarding it because this is our source of spiritual strength. In Isaiah 40:31 it says that "they that wait upon the Lord shall renew their strength; they shall mount up with wings as eagles; they shall run, and not be weary; and they shall walk and not faint."

The enemy knows this. He makes it his number one goal to distract us from our secret place. He will allow us to be busy with many things in our service to the Lord for as long as he can take us away from our secret place. He knows that this is where our spiritual power comes from. This is where we learn to win the battle against him and against our flesh. Every time we pray and spend time in the presence of God, we are being strengthened spiritually and we are being infused with power from on high. We are filled with the Holy Spirit and this is what makes us victorious over the wiles of the enemy.

The secret place is also our resting place. In Psalms 91:1; the psalmist declared that "He who dwells in the secret place of the most High shall abide under the shadow of the Almighty. This place is where we find rest and security. We dwell in it, like living in a house, we find shelter in His presence. It makes us safe from anyone who will try to destroy us.

How do we guard our secret place? There are several ways in which we can guard our secret place. First is **discipline**. If we do not discipline ourselves in this area, we will not be consistent with it and will eventually find ourselves not doing it. Paul talks about disciplining himself in I Cor. 9:26-27; "Therefore I do not run uncertainly (without definite aim). I do not box like one beating the air and striking without an adversary. But like a boxer, i buffet my body, handling it roughly, discipline it by hardships and subdue it." Second is that we must **stick to it**. Abiding is a recurring theme in God's recipe to help us stay in Him. To abide means to dwell and being consistently in attendance. To abide is to stay and tarry and to make our habitation in the place. Sticking with our set time of the day in meeting with God and checking in our secret place must be a priority to us. If we do not stick to it, it won't stick with us. We must do it whether we feel like it or not. The enemy will try to always distract us and keep us from shutting the door, but it is because he knows that is where our power lies. We must not succumb to the lies of the enemy. We must guard our secret place.

Another way on how we can guard our secret place is to *learn to wait*. Isaiah 40:31 says that those who wait upon the Lord shall renew their strength and power, they shall lift their wings and mount up close to God as eagles mount up to the sun, they shall run and not be weary, they shall walk and not faint or become tired. (Amplified)

What to guard in our secret place?

1. *Guard your heart.* Proverbs 4:23 says; "Keep and guard your heart with all vigilance and above all that you guard, for out of it flow the springs of life." Our hearts become a well of everything that the Lord gives to us in the secret place. The joy of the Lord, His peace, His wisdom, His known will, His ways all come to dwell richly in our hearts when we spend time with the Lord in prayer in the secret place. These become our treasures

which we should guard with all diligence. The enemy of our soul always seek to steal, kill and destroy. Guarding our hearts will allow us to keep everything that the Lord has given us in the secret place.

2.   *Guard His words.* Proverbs 4:20-21 says "My son, attend to my words, constantly submit to my sayings. Let them not depart from your sight; keep them in the centre of your heart." To keep something at the centre of our heart means to put it at the particularly important place so it's safe. To guard His words, His revelations, His teachings in our hearts is to be able to have a treasury where we can draw upon in time of need. The Holy Spirit can remind us of all these words and truths when we are being tempted by the enemy or going through trials in our lives.

Jesus also taught us to watch and pray. In Matthew 26:41, He said; "Watch and pray so that you will not fall into temptation. The spirit is willing, but the flesh is weak." In prayer, we also must learn to watch. The enemy will seek to prevent us from having quality time with the Lord. He will try to put different thoughts in our minds, lists of stuff to do, flashes of fleshly desires will come at the very point of prayer, but we must persevere to enter our secret place. Eventually, these distractions, these voices will die down and we can then get into the stillness of our soul. That is when we begin to wait upon the Lord. Prayer brings the atmosphere of heaven down. It is the greatest antidote for worldliness. We become more heavenly minded in prayer for we ascend to the heavenly realm every time we pray. Prayer is a transaction with God, witnessed in heaven watched in amazement by the angels of God. When we pray and when we couple it with fasting, it makes the things of the Spirit alive and clear. It gives us clearer vision, opening our spiritual eyes to see the things of the Spirit and gives us sharp ears to hear heaven and the voice of God within our soul.

Spiritual things and the supernatural are always alive and operating in the heavenly realm. We are just not in tune with it because of our lack of prayer. We see it vaguely and only glimpses of it because we do not pray. We do not make it a priority to dwell in the shadow of the Almighty. Therefore, we do not position ourselves to receive and to see. It takes prayer to open our eyes to see what is available to us. This can only be done in the secret place.

In 2 Kings 6:17 we can see Elisha praying for his servant Gehazi for him to see what the prophet could see in the spirit realm. "Then Elisha prayed and said, "Oh Lord, I pray, open his eyes that he may see." And the Lord opened the servant's eyes and he saw; and behold the mountain was full of horses and chariots of fire all around Elisha. This was when the King of Aram, an enemy of Israel sent his army to find and capture Elisha and they surrounded the city where Elisha lives. Gehazi was so afraid and wondered why his master Elisha was unmoved and seemingly at peace! Then Elisha said to him; "Do not be afraid, those who are with us are more than those who are with them." (2 Kings 6:16)

There is a place in the secret shadow of the Almighty where we find strength and courage. This is our personal time with God in the secret place we chose, where the door is always shut. We are alone with the living God. We must guard and protect it from anything that will clutter its existence from our everyday routine. It is in this place where we can find peace, rest for our souls and joy found in His presence alone.

...when you pray, go
into your room and
when you have shut
your door, pray to
your Father who is in
the secret place, and
your Father who sees
in secret will reward
you openly...

Matthew 6:6

9

The power of the secret place

Prayer does not fit us for the greater work. Prayer is the greater work.

Oswald Chambers

Satan cannot deny that great wonders have been wrought by prayer. As the spirit of prayer goes up, so his kingdom goes down.

William Gurnall

Much have been written about the power of prayer. We have all been taught about the indispensable nature of this discipline and yet we are all short of prayer. Majority of us still find it hard to shut the door. But the power of the secret place is undeniable. We only need to look back in history and watch men and women who have done great exploits for God during their lifetime. We can all attribute

71

their great success to the secret place. What lies behind the secret place? What power awaits those who discovered it and determined to shut the door and stay inside this mysterious dwelling?

The power of prayer is undeniable. Billy Graham said towards the end of his life in an interview that he wished he had prayed more. That if there is one thing, he would have changed over the course of his life it was that, he wished he spent more time in prayer. E. M. Bounds, one of the greatest American authors on prayer once said; "The men who have done the most for God in this world have been early on their knees." The power of prayer resonates in the lives of these men and women of God. They have discovered the power of prayer and lived it.

The secret place possesses the secret to victory over sin and the world. Two biggest temptations confronting us every day. If we are much with God and stay and wait in the secret place to commune with God, we will receive the strength and the power that we need to say no to Satan's many attempts to distract us and tempt us to sin or choose the ways of the world rather than God's righteous ways. The power to live a holy life belongs in the secret place.

What more, but we all know that the presence of God rubbing upon our existence can bring the power of heaven everywhere we go. Our lives will be making an impact to others because every day we spend time in the presence of God in the secret place. People will notice the difference. Your face will be shining. There will be an unexplainable glow in your countenance. Moses, after spending 40 days and forty nights on the mountain in the presence of God came down and His face was radiant. The Israelites could not stand to look at him because they were dazzled by his shining face! God's holiness and radiance rubbed on him!

Jesus Himself demonstrated the power of prayer. Before any ministry each day, he would spend time on the mountain or in the wilderness or in a garden to be with the Heavenly Father. To receive from Him the day's assignment. He walked with God constantly that He was always in step with the Father. This is an example he left us with from His own life. The power comes from the daily prayer time He spent with the Father in the secret place.

The early apostles, when the work of ministry was expanding

thought it unwise to be distracted from their secret place to attend to the demands of ministry. They said in Acts 6:2; "Then the twelve called the multitude of the disciples unto them and said, "It would not be right for us to neglect the ministry of the word of God in order to wait on tables. Brothers and sisters choose seven men from among you who are known to be full of the Holy Spirit and wisdom. We will turn this responsibility over to them and will give our attention to *prayer and the ministry of the word.*"

Remember that in the prayer closet, you have two disciplines: Prayer and reading the Word of God. These two are the building blocks of a successful Christian life. Aside from these two, there will be no other that can equal in importance. The enemy will try to take you away from these two disciplines which is essentially neglecting your secret place. In prayer you learn to worship which is our first calling in life. God inhabits our praises (Psalms 22:3) He literally comes into our hearts and work inside our soul through worship. That is how we know we are in the presence of God and it's very powerful!

The power of the secret place comes to us like a daily bread from heaven. Without it, we will be spiritually malnourished and even sick! Our spiritual health depends on it. If you are keeping this discipline and does not let the enemy distract you from it, then you have discovered the secret to a powerful Christian life and this will not be taken away from you.

The power of the secret place and all that awaits us in this place I'd summarised beautifully in this quote by E.M. Bounds in his book, "The Weapon of Prayer"

"Men and women are needed whose prayers will give to the world the utmost power of God, who will make His promises to blossom with rich and full results. God is waiting to hear us and challenges us to bring Him to do this thing by our praying. He is asking us today, as He did His ancient Israel, to prove Him now herewith." Behind God's Word is God Himself, and we read:
"Thus, saith the Lord, the Holy One of Israel, his Maker: Ask of me things to come and concerning my sons, and concerning the work of my hands, command ye me." As though God places Himself in the hands and at the disposal of His people who pray- as indeed He does. The dominant element of all praying is faith, that is conspicuous, cardinal and emphatic. Without such faith it is impossible to please God, and equally impossible to pray.

BUT ONE THNG IS NEEDFUL: AND MARY HATH
CHOSEN THAT GOOD PART, WHICH SHALL
NOT BE TAKEN AWAY FROM HER.

LUKE 10:42

10

Only one thing is needed

You are worried and upset about many things, but only one thing is needed.

Luke 10:41-42

In this incredibly famous account of Jesus visiting Martha and Mary's home, we all can get a glimpse of our own busy existence. Each of us can indeed identify with Martha who was worried and troubled about many things. It is typical of living in this hectic, modern world. Then we see Mary on the other side and wonder at the seeming simplicity of what she chose to do during Martha's never-ending distractions. She seated herself at the Lord's feet and was listening to His teachings.

This account reflected two different worlds. The world of Martha represented the world for almost all of us.

The world with all its distractions and demands which call upon us, demanding our immediate attention every single day. Then we have the world of Mary, a less hurried, peaceful existence, who, as Jesus has pointed out was the better world. Mary has chosen the good portion which shall not be taken away from her.

This is a profound teaching. What was Mary doing in the story if we compared her to her sister Martha? Nothing! Martha was doing all the serving. In fact, she couldn't stand it any longer, it seemed very unfair, so she went to Jesus and said, "Lord, is it nothing to you that my sister has left me to serve alone? Tell her then to help me (to lend a hand and do her part along with me)! (Amplified)

Many times, we choose the world of Martha because the flesh wants to be doing something all the time. We thrive in activities and constant engagements. To be occupied is the name of the game. If our diary isn't full, we get restless. So much so that some of us even need to have a personal assistant to sort out our hectic diaries! There is no room in our schedule to stand still. We are bombarded by calls, emails, information sent to us via Facebook, Twitter, what's up, viber and Instagram. We are constantly fed with information of all sorts from all kinds of social media vehicle. Our heads are buzzing with thoughts all the time. This is the modern world of Martha in which we live. As a result, we are chronically worried and upset about so many things.

This was the picture that Jesus hoped to bring to the attention of Martha and to us who had to live and fight the tyranny of being busy. Mary in her simplicity found the one thing that is needful. She was in the presence of Jesus and nothing could be more important than listening to the words of Jesus, feeding with the bread of life and drinking the living water. These were the eternal things. Jesus said whoever eats the bread that He will give will never be hungry again and whoever drinks the water He will give will never be thirsty again. He is laying it down to everyone that only He can satisfy the longings of our hearts. When we find it, it will never be taken away from us. It will end all our search, so much so that we would be willing to sell everything we have, to possess it. This is the better portion which Mary has chosen, and Jesus said to her that it will not be taken away from her.

The one thing that is needful. Many of us try to pursue too many things in this life. The call of Jesus for us to learn to shut the door means that we must learn to leave behind what worries us so that we can focus on Him when we are in the secret place. His invitation was "Come to me, all of you who are weary and carry heavy burdens, and I will give you rest. Take my yolk upon you and learn from me, for I am gentle and humble in heart, and you will find rest for your souls." (Matthew 11:28-29)

When Jesus said to us "Seek first the kingdom of God and His righteousness and all these things shall be added unto us"; he is talking about the one thing needed that we must learn to seek first in this life. To pursue heavenly things, those that will last and have eternal values. The words of God, they are our bread of life, Jesus said; "Man shall not live by bread alone but by every Word that comes out of the mouth of God". When we spend time with the Lord, we hear His words and His presence becomes alive to us. He Himself is the Word, Jesus said, He is the living bread. His presence, His joy, His peace become ours when we tarry in the secret place. He is the one thing that is needful, He is our pearl of great price. For Him, we would gladly sell everything that we have in order to have Him. He becomes to us the most important person in our lives. Worthy of our undivided attention and focus. This is what it means to seek the face of God and to behold His glory. When we are studying the Word of God, it is as if we are beholding His glory for the Bible is all about the glory of God. When we pray, the Holy Spirit makes the presence of Christ real to us. His presence gives us life and joy, a satisfaction not found anywhere else. This is the one thing needed. It will not be taken away from us.

FOR WE WRESTLE NOT AGAINST FLESH AND
BLOOD, BUT AGAINST PRINCIPALITIES,
AGAINST POWER, AGAINST THE RULERS OF
THE DARKNESS OF THIS WORLD, AGAINST
SPIRITUAL WICKEDNESS IN HIGH PLACES.

EPHESIAN 6:12

11

Lockdowns in history

What the church needs today is not more machinery or better, not new organisations or more and novel methods, but men whom the Holy Ghost can use- men of prayer, men mighty in prayer...

E.M. Bounds

Great men and women in history showed us that spending time alone with God can be immensely powerful. They were ordinary people who have learned to pray and shut their doors. They were the ones who have discovered the unspeakable joy found in the secret place. They have known what it was like to have the unlimited resources of heaven at their disposal. They knew what it was like to take hold of God and showed us that to take God at His Word was what it meant to live by faith. History has blessed us with such men and women. We are blessed to have seen their footprints left for us to follow. We can indeed heed the lessons taught by each of their lives as we seek to find our own secret place with God. May their journey help us and may their dedication challenge us to pursue God's higher purpose for our lives. In the secret place of the Most High God.

David Brainerd

I got hold of David Brainerd's diary, in a book entitled; "The Life and Diary of David Brainerd" when I was just in high school. At the time, I was already practicing daily devotions and spending quiet times with the Lord on a regular basis. But something in his diary has affected my soul. It made a lasting impression on me. It was the deep devotion found in all his entries. His love for God was palpable in every page. Here was a young man in his twenties who have known the love of God in a profound way. David Brainerd was a missionary to the Native Americans particularly the Delaware Indians in the 1700's. He was an intelligent young man, a student of Yale University and was well known by Jonathan Edwards who commented on how talented and well-spoken the man was. He was particularly noted to be a wonderful conversationalist. And yet it was his prayer life that has made a lasting impression among the Indians he wanted to reach. The Delaware Indians were a ferocious tribe. F. W. Boreham recorded an incident when David was about to enter the Indian community to preach the Gospel to them. Without his knowledge, his every move was being watched by the warriors sent out to kill him. But when they got closer to Brainerd's tent, they saw the paleface on his knees. And as he prayed, suddenly a rattlesnake slipped to his side, lifted up its ugly head to strike, flicked its fork tongue almost in his face, and then without any apparent reason, glided swiftly away into the brushwood. "The Great Spirit" is with the paleface!" The Indians said, and thus they accorded him a prophet's welcome. He was revered among them as the "Prophet of God" because of this incident as clearly recorded by F.W. Boreham.

Many entries in his diary were about the time he spent with the Lord in prayer. Sometimes he would write that he spent the entire day from morning till night in secret fasting and prayer! His short ministry was characterised with mighty revivals and awakenings among the Indians. He wrote of many souls being saved and how the Indians would flock to the door of his tent asking in tears about how they can be saved! David was a very frail young man who suffered with tuberculosis and yet the Lord has mightily used his life for the salvation of many. His life inspired modern missionary movement and his diary challenged countless would be missionaries to give their lives to Christ. The power of the secret place cannot be demonstrated any greater than in the life of this young missionary.

Father Nash, the man behind Charles Finney's success

For most of us, we only heard of Charles Finney and his successful revival stories. But behind this recorded history is a less known story of a man who spent many agonising hours in the secret place interceding for the preacher and for souls while Charles Finney was preaching to the people.

A story was told that Father Nash would often go before Charles Finney to the community where they would have the revival meeting and there rent a place where he could pray and intercede for a few weeks prior to the meetings. He would ask one or two prayer warriors in the community to join him in praying for the outpouring of the Holy Spirit in the community before Charles Finney came to speak. One story was told of a woman who was the owner of the cottage where they rented to pray, asking Charles to come and check on the men inside the room for they haven't had anything to eat since they arrived. That was already three days ago. She described them as groaning and was worried that something is going on with them. Charles then reassured her that the men were only in travail praying for souls! The power wrought in prayer cannot be understated. Here, it was indispensable. No other power can bring down heaven to us if we are truly seeking revival, than the power of prayer in the secret place.

George Whitefield

Throughout his ministry, George Whitefield was devoted to prayer and personal experience with the Holy Spirit. He often wrote in his journal, encounters with the Holy Spirit and the joy and peace that came to him every time. He was indeed a powerful preacher, passionate for God and His Word and yet the very secret to this power lies in his disciplined prayer life. There were many nights of prayer mentioned in his journal and alongside John Wesley, he was one of the most influential evangelists of his time.

John Wesley

John Wesley was the founder of Methodism. At the time of his ministry, he was a layman who was not allowed to preach within the organised church. So, he started preaching outside the walls of the established churches of his day. Along with George Whitfield, he was also a man of prayer and an avid student of the word of God. It has been said that John Wesley often study even whilst on horseback! He was a man who will not waste any time. He also once said that he thought little of a man who did not pray four hours every day. He himself would rise at 4 am every day to seek God for the first four hours of the day. In his later years, he was known to spend 8 hours in prayer!

He left us with a powerful quote on prayer found in his book; How to Pray: The best of John Wesley on Prayer: "In using all means, seek God alone. In and through every outward thing, look only to the power of His Spirit, and the merits of His Son. Beware you do not get stuck in the work itself; if you do it is all lost labour. Nothing short of God can satisfy your soul. Therefore, fix on Him, in all, through all, and above all... Remember also to use all means as means- as ordained, not for their own sake..."

Behind John Wesley's success in ministry was his disciplined prayer life. He allowed himself to be in lockdowns with God. He guarded his secret place jealously, first and foremost. And yet, behind his life was a praying mother, Susana Wesley who used to pray two hours each day under an apron to signal to everyone at home, she is spending time with the Lord and not to be disturbed! There inside the spread of an apron, she would allow herself to be in lockdown with God, praying, interceding for her husband and for her children and studying the Word of God. The fruit of her prayerful life was evident in the lives of John Wesley and even Charles Wesley, his brother. He wrote many inspiring hymns for the Christian church in their generation which we still use to this day.

Hudson Taylor

Like John Wesley's background, Hudson Taylor's life was also the result of a mother's prayerful life. His own mother prayed and interceded for his conversion. This has happened at the very time of his surrender to the finish work of Christ, there, alone at his father's library, reading a gospel tract and his mother, many miles away in prevailing intercession for his salvation. His life was an extension of the life of his praying mother. The power of prayer was seen in many accounts of his life in countless answers to prayers even to the smallest matter in which He tested the promises of God to be true. He takes God at His Word and has lived the reality of the promises in his own life and ministry. This was the legacy he left of which his son, Dr Howard Taylor was most impressed with. In the book "Hudson Taylor's Spiritual Secret" (p.243), Howard remembered a night travelling with his father through China. He writes, "It was not easy for Mr. Taylor in his changeful life, to make time for prayer and Bible Study, but he knew that it was vital. Well do the writers remember travelling with him month after month in northern China, by cart and wheelbarrow, with the poorest of inns at night. Often with only one large room for coolies and travellers alike, they would screen off a corner for their father and another for themselves, with curtains of some sort; and then after sleep at last had brought a measure of quiet they would hear a match struck and seek a flicker of candlelight which told that Mr. Taylor, however weary, was pouring over the little bible in two volumes always at hand. From two to four a.m. was the time he usually gave to prayer; the time when he could be most sure of being undisturbed to wait upon God. That flicker of candlelight has meant more to them than all they have read or heard on secret prayer; it meant reality, not preaching but practice."

D. L. Moody

In his book, "Why God used D.L. Moody, R.A Torrey described the secret life of prayer of the man who has accomplished so much in his lifetime. D. L. Moody was a well-known American evangelist whose legacy was felt for many generations to come. He conducted powerful revival meetings, founded the Moody Bible. institute in Chicago, established a publishing business, started the Moody church, and has personally led countless souls to the saving knowledge of Jesus Christ. It has been said that he will not let a single day pass without talking to someone about Christ.

R. A. Torrey was a close confidante of D. L. Moody. He became a friend he would trust his deepest secret.

Torrey testified in his book about D. L. Moody's powerful prayer life. He said that D.L. Moody was more of a praying man than he was a preacher. He said of the man; "Time and time again, he was confronted by obstacles that seemed insurmountable, but he always knew the way to surmount and to overcome all difficulties. He knew the way to bring to pass anything that needed to be brought to pass. He knew and believe in the deepest depths of his soul that "nothing was too hard for the Lord" and that prayer could do anything that

God could do." There were many nights of prayer even with the students in the Bible Schools at his urgings.

There were fasting and waiting upon the Lord for His blessings to come. Both financial difficulties and problems with difficult people were solved by prayers. He obtained direct answers to his many prayers in the same way he asked the Lord specifically. Torrey commented that Moody was a man who believed in the God who answers prayer and not only believed in Him in a theoretical way but believed in Him in a practical way. He was a man who met every difficulty that stood in his way - by prayer. Everything he undertook was backed up by prayer and in everything, his ultimate dependence was upon God.

The Lewis sisters who prayed down revival

Within the backdrop of spiritual dryness and apathy, two aged sisters in the island of Lewis in the Hebrides, Scotland were burdened to pray for revival in their small village called Barvas. They sensed the Lord speaking to them; "I will pour water on the thirsty land, and streams on the dry ground." (Isaiah 44:3)

At the beginning of November 1949, Peggy, and Christine Smith, 84 and 82 years old-Peggy, completely blind, and Christine bent over with arthritis started praying in their small cottage two or three nights per week from 10 pm till 3 am. After several weeks of praying, Peggy had a vision of her church being crowded with young people and an unknown minister preaching from the pulpit.

Peggy then told their minister, Rev. James McKay that they sensed that the Lord is about to send revival and that he must get his church leaders to pray every Tuesday and Friday night while they too will be praying in their cottage.

The minister respected the sister's request and the call to pray was made. There was also a group of pastors in the region that met to discuss the growing spiritual declension in the island, and they started an appeal for all believers to view with concern the barrenness of the parishes so they would turn again to the Lord whom they have grieved with their waywardness and iniquities. They also asked the people to pray for the spirit of repentance to visit the island. This appeal was read to parishes and placed in the two newspapers: The Stornoway Gazette and West coast advisor on the 9th of December 1949.

Following that proclamation, two times per week, Peggy and Christine prayed in their cottage from 10 pm till 3 am while ministers also pray in other locations. People all over the islands sensed that God was telling them to "ask me for revival" which they did so desperately, praying even in unheated buildings during the winter months.

After several weeks of praying like that, one evening, while the minister and church leaders were praying in a barn, a young deacon read from Psalms 24:3-5.

Who shall ascend into the hill of the Lord?
Or who shall stand in His Holy presence?
He that hath clean hands and a pure heart, who hath not lifted his soul into vanity, nor sworn deceitfully.
He shall receive the blessing from the Lord, and righteousness from the God of his salvation.

When he closed his bible, he looked at the minister and the others and said "It seems to me to be so much humbug to be praying as we are praying to be waiting as we are waiting, if we ourselves are not rightly related to God." He then prayed, "God, are my hands clean? Is my heart pure?"

Immediately at around 3 am the presence of God gripped

every person present. It was not only them, but the entire village and the surrounding areas felt the same awareness of God. The following day everyone was absorbed by the reality of eternal things. Revival broke out!

That group of intercessors left the barn at that early hour and found men and women kneeling along the roads, crying out to God for mercy. Every home had lights on in it, as no one could sleep with the awareness of God being so overwhelming.

Peggy Smith then sent for her minister and told him that he was supposed to invite someone to come and preach during the revival, but she did not know who he was. She only saw an unfamiliar face in the vision.

Through another contact McKay invited Duncan Campbell and asked him to come but he was unable to come because he was in the middle of an evangelistic campaign on the island of Skye with many conversions taking place. He replied to Rev. MacKay's letter explaining the situation. The minister regretfully told Peggy that Mr. Duncan Campbell could not come to which Peggy replied, "Mr. McKay, that is what man is saying. But God has said something else and he will be here within a fortnight."

Due to a change of events, the convention on Skye was cancelled and Campbell arrived on the island of Lewis in ten days. He was about to witness one of the greatest revivals in the history of the island.

I can go on and on and we won't have space to mention Charles Spurgeon, Oswald Chambers who said "Shut out every other consideration and keep yourself before God for this one thing only- My Utmost for His Highest. I am determined to be absolutely and entirely for Him and for Him alone."; Reece Howells who was a well-known intercessor during World War 2, missionary greats like David Livingstone, Adoniram Hudson, Henry Martyn, Count Nicolaus Ludwig Von Zinzendorf who said; "I have but one passion: It is He, it is He alone. The world is the field and the field is the world; and henceforth that country shall be my home where I can be most used in winning souls for Christ."

Throughout history, God has raised men and women who discovered the power of the secret place. They allowed themselves to be in lockdown with God and emerged victorious influencing their generation and inspiring faith.

Alone with God

By: Marivic Quiazon

Alone with God, I must
To behold His love so vast
There's joy in every gaze
As I look upon His face.

This grace I know like Moses did
When alone with God He walked
Like Enoch and Noah before Him
He knew the God I long to know.

There in the wilderness
Or desert one must cross
No place too far, no mountain too high
Alone with God, I must remain.

Heroes of faith, we heard of them
Like Abraham who trusted God
No reservation, he fully knew
The God of heaven, he obeyed.

Men of God, women of God
Renowned because of faith so bold
God's book records the path they trod
Their courage marked by blood.

12

Biblical lockdowns

And what shall I more say? for the time would fail me
to tell of Gideon, and Barack, and of Samson, and of
Jepthae: of David also, and Samuel, and of the
prophets: who through faith subdued kingdoms,
wrought righteousness, obtained promises, stopped
the mouths of lions. Quenched the violence of fire,
escaped the edged of the sword, out of weakness were
made strong, waxed valiant in fight, turned to fight
the armies of the aliens.

Hebrews 11: 32 -34 (KJV)

There were many men and women in the Bible who

went into lockdown with God before God used them
mightily. These were men and women whose faith were tried

and tested by fire. Like pure diamonds, they have been through much purification before they turned into priceless stones. I believe that God uses lockdown to allow us to experience Him deeper. To prune and purge us and purify our faith. This sharpening can happen in our times alone with God and it will not be any different from the lockdowns we can see recorded in God's Holy Book.

Enoch

Enoch- a man who walked with God..

"*And Enoch walked with God: and he was not; for God took Him." (Genesis 5:24)*

Here, we see a man who learned to walk with God, to be in close fellowship with him in his lifetime that God prevented him from dying, he took him up! In Hebrews 11:5 we read;

"By faith Enoch was taken up so that he should not see death, and he was not found because God had taken him". Before he was taken, it was said of him that he was a man who pleased God. He walked with Him every day of his life. This is ultimately what staying and living in the secret place is like. It is living in close relationship with the Lord, like Enoch did. Walking with God daily means having a daily fellowship with the Lord, honouring Him in our daily life, including Him in our decisions, submitting to His will, seeking His will every time more than our will. This is the life of faith that pleases God.

Noah

"And Noah did all that the Lord commanded him.

Noah was six hundred years old when the floodwaters came on the earth. And Noah and his sons and his wife and his son's wives entered the ark to escape the waters of the flood. (Genesis 7: 5-7 NIV)

Noah and his family together with all kinds of paired animals went into lockdown staying inside the ark for a total of 150 days. It must have been difficult for them hearing the cries of those perishing in the flood whilst inside the ark. But the Lord's presence must be inside the ark teaching them His salvation and love. They were saved because they were found righteous in their generation compared to the rest of the world who abandoned the fear of God and chose to live for themselves. Lockdown inside the ark, Noah and his family were safe and secure. Sometimes, when God choose to put us in lockdown, though it will not be comfortable, it will definitely be for our good in the end.

Joseph

Joseph was not unfamiliar with lockdowns. Twice, he was placed in this kind of situation. First in the pit by his brothers who threw him there. Second was when Potiphar's wife tried to seduce him and when he won't give in, she made up a story and accused him of trying to rape her. He was thrown into prison because of this injustice. He experienced two kinds

of injustice leading to him entering lockdowns. Yet, he was not alone. In all these, the Lord was with Joseph. We read an account of this Genesis 39:19-21 (New Living Translation) "Potiphar was furious when he heard his wife's story about how Joseph had treated her. So, he took Joseph and threw him into prison where the king's prisoners were held, and there he remained. But the Lord was with Joseph in the prison and showed him His faithful love. And the Lord made Joseph a favourite with the prison warden."

When the Lord is with us, all kinds of favour will come our way. It is because the hand of the Lord brings protection and blessings wherever we are. Lockdowns enable us to see that the Lord makes all things beautiful in His time. It teaches us to wait on the Lord. It teaches us patience and stillness. The voice of the Lord is heard. Joseph learned to trust the Lord who works all things together for the good of those who love Him and are called according to His purpose. (Romans 8:28)

Moses

"Moses remained there on the mountain with the Lord forty days and forty nights. In all that time, he ate no bread and drank no water. And the Lord wrote the terms of the covenant- the Ten Commandments- on the stone tablets.
(Exodus 34:28,
New Living Translation)

Moses is probably one of the most talked about biblical character we know. He was commended by the Lord as the most humble and meekest man who ever lived.

Jesus stressed this truth when He said, "Come unto me, all you who are weary and burdened and I will give you rest. Take my yolk upon you and learn from me for I am meek and lowly in heart, and you will find rest for your souls." (Matthew 11:28-29, NIV/ KJV)

Spending time with the Lord will allow us to learn from his heart, meekness, and humility. His heart is tender and very gentle and indeed as we spend time with Him, these characteristics will rub off on us! We become like the person we hang out with all the time! Couples who have been together for a long time sometimes resemble each other. This is also true in the spiritual sense. Our character will grow to be more like Jesus as we spend more time with Him each day. Moses learned how to be meek because he spent time with the Lord each day and longer! He started out as a short-tempered young man from being a prince from Egypt, killing an Egyptian and staying in the wilderness. He had learned from God humility and gentleness. He fasted forty days and forty nights twice in his lifetime both during the giving of the Ten Commandments. The first time, he ended up destroying the tablet of stone where the commandments were written because of the sin of the people of Israel. Then the second time he had to go up to the mountain again and fast forty days and forty nights as the Lord did the writing of the Ten Commandments again. He was in extended lockdown a few times! At one point he came down from the mountain with his face shining brightly and the people could not look on him! The holiness and glory of the Lord rubbed off on him! Talked about resemblance!

To be more like Christ in character and desires, we ought to spend regular time with Him and if called upon, we must be ready to allow an extended time alone with the Lord. This is extremely important as we seek His face and desire to know Him deeper in our lives.

Joshua

"Inside the Tent of Meeting, the Lord would speak to Moses face to face, as one speaks to a friend. Afterward Moses would return to the camp, but the young man who assisted him, Joshua, son of Nun, would remain behind the Tent of Meeting." (Exodus 33:11)

Joshua was Moses assistant during their time in the wilderness. Being an assistant, he would accompany Moses most of time to wherever he would go. This will include his meetings with God Himself up in Mt. Sinai or within the tabernacle or the Tent of Meeting. Here, he would learn the value of the secret place, of spending time alone with God. All these were part of his preparation to be the next leader to lead Israel to the promised land. His internship under the instructions of Moses was significant. God used it to develop in him a heart fully devoted and committed to following God. He learned from Moses and Aaron the importance of prayer in winning the battle. We see in Exodus 17:8-16; how he won the battle with Amalek through the power of prayer. In front of him fighting the Amalekites were Moses lifting his staff to God. When he gets tired, Aaron and Hur will support his arms. If Moses' arms were up in prayer, Joshua was winning the battle. When it was down, Joshua was losing the battle. From here, Joshua would learn the most important lesson in leadership: Dependence on God alone.

We also see an occasion when the seventy elders of Israel, Joshua, included, along with Moses, Aaron, Nadab and Abihu were called to join God on Mt. Sinai. They had worship and covenant meal in God's presence, but Moses took Joshua with him further up on the mountain and spent another six days with the Lord in the mountain. On the seventh day, Moses left him alone for forty days in the mountain! That must have been a powerful lockdown experience with God. This probably contributed to his love for the secret place, his desire for God's presence as whenever he was with Moses in the Tent of Meeting, he would stay behind to also be in God's presence longer.

Earlier on in Joshua's life, we see how the Lord took him aside, alongside Moses, to prepare him for leadership. Joshua did great exploits for God but on giving advice to the Israelites who will go with him to the promised land, he gave an incredibly wise advice which we can always take with us:

"This book of the law shall not depart from your mouth, but you shall meditate in it day and night, that you may observe to do according to all that is written in it. For then you will make your way prosperous, and you will have good success." (Joshua 1:8)

Nehemiah

"When I heard these things, I sat down and wept. For some days I mourned and fasted and prayed before the God of heaven. Then I said: "Lord, the God of heaven, the great and awesome God, who keeps his covenant of love with those who love Him and keep his commandments, let your ear be attentive and your eyes open to hear the prayer your servant is praying before you day and night.... (Nehemiah 1:4-6, NIV)

The book of Nehemiah started with this powerful lockdown prayer... of a mighty intercession for the people of Israel who were remnants, who had survived the exile and now were occupying Jerusalem in great disgrace and trouble because the wall of Jerusalem was greatly destroyed.

Nehemiah was a man of action who knew God. He cared for the honour of His name. This ordinary man accomplished great things for God because he was also a man of prayer. He knew what to do in times of distress. He chose to lock himself before God prior to doing anything to face the mountain of trouble before him. He chose to be in lockdown with God. Here was an example of a choice we can all make to enter a season of lockdown with God for a purpose. You might be encountering a huge setback in your business, a problem that seems impossible to solve, a huge mountain to overcome, incurable disease or a great danger requiring supernatural intervention. This can be your best option. Go out into the woods, close the door and be inside your room, go up to the mountain, go somewhere where you can be alone with your God, choose to enter a season of lockdown like what Nehemiah did and seek God's grace for your situation, ask for His favour and allow Him to show you great and mighty things which you do not know! Jeremiah 33:3 says, "Call unto me and I will answer you and show you great and mighty things which you do not know."

Nehemiah's lockdown resulted in great exploits, changing the course of history for the Jewish people who have returned from exile. Rebuilding the walls of Jerusalem was not an easy task. Yet, because of heaven's intervention, the task was accomplished in the face of even the hardest oppositions! This can only be done through prayer. Oh, the power of prayer! If we can only give ourselves to prayer, nothing will be impossible to us.

Samuel

The boy Samuel ministered before the Lord under Eli. In those days the word of the Lord was rare; there were not many visions. One night, Eli whose eyes were becoming so weak that he could barely see, was lying down in his usual place. The lamp of God had not yet gone out, and Samuel was lying down in the temple of the Lord, where the ark of God was. Then the Lord called Samuel. Samuel answered, "Here I am."

Samuel's life was an answer to a fervent prayer of his mother, Hannah. She prayed for a child and Samuel was the answer and a promise she made if God would answer her prayers. She promised to give Samuel to the Lord. She did this and brought him to the temple as soon as he was weaned. Samuel was growing up in the presence of the Lord. In I Samuel 2:18 we read; "But Samuel, though he was only a boy, served the Lord. He wore a linen garment like that of a priest." (NLT)

Here was a record of the longest lockdown in the Bible. Samuel was in lockdown with the Lord as he was growing up. He was ministering to the Lord, sleeping every night near the ark of the covenant where the presence of God dwells! What an awesome place to live! Samuel knew God intimately and has grown to recognise the voice of God.

David

"In the morning, oh Lord, you will hear my voice; in the morning I will order my prayer to you

and eagerly watch." (Psalms 5:3, NAS)

David was known to be a man of prayer. He was called by God to be a man after God's own heart. Growing as a shepherd, he learned to wake up early in the morning and enjoy the presence of God whilst tending to his sheep. He learned from an early age how to enter the presence of the Lord. Reading the book of Psalms can give us a glimpse of his prayer life. He ordered his prayer from thanksgiving and praise to depending completely on the One who truly controls everything. His dependence upon the Lord can be seen when he fought Goliath in confidence and defeated him. He has no fear because he knew His God. Psalms is a book of praise and worship. It is like a prayer diary of David. We read his conversations with God, the longings of his heart, his struggles and his joy in the Lord. Everything that he felt was recorded in the book. His prayers were a mixture of praise, intimate worship and spirit led petitions and declaration coupled with prophecies into the future. One can see a rich prayer life of a man whose heart has been whole towards God just by reading the book of Psalms.

Jonah

"Then Jonah prayed to the Lord his God from the belly of the fish...." (Jonah 2:1, ESV)

The story of Jonah was something we can all relate to. Cornered by the Lord, he was forced into lockdown inside the belly of a big fish because he would not obey. There are times when we wanted to do our own will instead of what the Lord clearly is leading us to do.

When we messed up and has been stubborn, sometimes the only way for us to learn and eventually "wake up" is when we come to the end of our game and become helpless or bankrupt. When we tried to do things our way, we end up being placed in lockdown so that we can reflect on what we are doing and eventually return to the Lord, just like what Jonah did. From out of the belly of the fish, after three days, he learned to pray and obey God's command.

Sometimes it takes this kind of drastic measure for God to get our attention. We also learned from Jonah's story that we can never escape God's calling upon our lives. We will always be brought back to a place where we needed to confront this calling. God's call upon my life was noticeably clear. I knew it even when I was just twelve years old. I did not know what it was, but I knew I've got an assignment from God which my life must accomplish before it ends. Even when I have been to many roads in this life, it has never left me. I was forced to seriously confront this call in an unlikely place. I was a nurse looking after a patient who was dying. It was 2002, I can still vividly remember the look in my patient's eyes when he told me that he was not ready. That he did not want to die because he has not done what he was supposed to do in his life. That look was like a wakeup call to my heart. I kept delaying following God's call upon my life for years. I was young and has many plans. But the Lord spoke to me through that patient. I told Him I do not want to be in my death bed regretting that I have not done what He was asking my life to do. I came home that day and resolved to follow the Lord. And I have not looked back.

In Jonah's lockdown inside the belly of a big fish, he learned a valuable lesson about obedience... the hard way. He is a very peculiar prophet indeed! Even after preaching to Nineveh and seeing the people repenting, it displeased him because he felt that the people deserved to be punished because of their evil ways. So again, the Lord had to teach him a lesson about mercy using the withering of a gourd. (Jonah 4:5-11)

Jonah's unwillingness for the Ninevites to repent and be saved was something questionable of a prophet. It sounded not fitting for a prophet to be unconcerned about the lost and the kingdom of God. He seemed to still harbour a proud heart, not knowing God's love for sinners. In dealing with him, we saw God's wonderful patience towards him and his great mercy being extended to all men.

Isaiah

"In the year that king Uzziah died I saw also the Lord sitting upon a throne, high and lifted up, and his train filled the temple." (Isaiah 6:1, KJV)

At the time of King Uzziah's death, Isaiah must be feeling down and shattered. The country had no leader, and everything hangs in the balance about their future. During times of dejection, we tend to seek solace in prayer and most of the time more inclined to spend time alone with the Lord. God may use these times to lock us down in his presence and reveal himself to us. A seeking heart will always find God. Isaiah was no exception. He was seeking an answer at the time of uncertainty. In this account, the Lord chose to show Himself to Isaiah. The vision that the Lord gave Isaiah caused him to see himself for who he is and with his own eyes understand the holiness of God. Each of us must see God with our own eyes. We must know Christ personally to have a relationship with Him. We should not depend on others telling us about the Lord.

We must know the God of the Bible. We must know the God of our father. We should not be content with listening to stories of people who knew their God. We must have our own stories of God's mercy and forgiveness. Of tasting and seeing that the Lord is good. We must personally know God. During Isaiah's lockdown with God, he saw the Lord, His holiness and love as He cleansed his lips, symbolising forgiveness of sins. Then Isaiah heard the voice of the Lord calling him to go for Him to give warning and message to the

people of Israel. It must be quite an assignment! God works in mysterious ways and most of the time it is during our times alone with God, in the secret place that He reveals His will to us.

Daniel

"Now when Daniel learned that the decree had been published, he went home to his upstairs room where the window opened towards Jerusalem. Three times a day he got down on his knees and prayed, giving thanks to his God, just as he had done before." (Daniel 6:10, NIV)

Daniel's habit of entering his secret place with God caused him to be thrown into the lion's den as a punishment according to the decree ordered by King Darius. The king, at the suggestion of those people who hated Daniel and his friends ordered everyone under him to not worship or pray to any God except him.

When Daniel heard this, there was not a trace of fear or anger in him, instead he went about his prayer like he used to do three times a day. Here, we see a disciplined man when it comes to his prayers. Nothing is more important to him than this habit. He goes every day to his secret place and have communion with the God of heaven. We all know the end of this story as Daniel was spared by the Lord from the lion's den. The power of prayer was evident in this young man's life. In fact, he was so trustworthy that the Lord entrusted to him the vision of what is to come in the last days. If we know the Lord and understand His ways, we will grow into being a trustworthy servant. He will be able to trust us with his plans and purposes, kingdom related assignments and many souls who can be saved through the example of our lives.

John the Baptist

"And the child (John) grew and became strong in spirit, and he lived in the wilderness until he appeared publicly to Israel." (Luke 1:80, NIV)

Also, among one of the longest lockdowns with God, we see the account of John the Baptist's life as one of mystery and intrigue. He was born of an elderly couple, Zechariah, and Elizabeth. God told them both what name they will give the child. When Zechariah's tongue was released after the circumcision of John, and that it was time to name the baby, (his tongue was tied and he became mute because he laughed and doubted when God announced to him that He will give him a child in his old age and that he is to name him John), he uttered the name John to the astonishment of the neighbours. Clearly the Lord's hand was upon the boy. He grew up differently. He lived in the wilderness in lockdown with God. Here, he was trained by the Lord before he starts his remarkable ministry. His work is pivotal to the soon coming of the Messiah. He was the way maker. He prepared the way for the coming of Jesus, who is the Christ. He was also the first prophet to preach to Israel again after Malachi and it was 400 years of silence. No words from the Lord was heard during this silent year. Then came John the Baptist. His time with the Lord in the wilderness prepared him for such a great task ahead. He was courageous and never compromised his message. He was truly a man of God in every sense, like Elijah in many ways. He came and fulfilled his work after being in lockdown in the wilderness and God was with him.

Paul

"But when He who had set me apart before I was born, and who called me by His grace, was pleased to reveal His Son to me, in order that I might preach Him among the Gentiles, I did not]

immediately consult with anyone; nor did I go up to Jerusalem to those who were apostles before me, but I went away into Arabia, and returned again to Damascus. Then

after three years I went up to Jerusalem to visit Cephas and remained with him fifteen days." (Galatians 1:15-18, ESV)

Paul, one of the greatest apostles who ever lived was seen here giving an account of his three years in lockdown with God in the desert of Arabia. Bible historians speculates that this place could be in the East of Jordan and it might have been during this time where Paul learned much from Jesus Himself in preparation for his preaching to the Gentiles. The necessity of being taken aside to be prepared for a great task is not uncommon in the Bible. We see a God who takes His time to prepare his chosen people. Lockdowns are necessary to shape our character, prepare our hearts to be humble and pure and to make us bold and strong. To be like Christ, we must know Him. And there is no other way of knowing Him, except to shut the door behind us and enter our secret place with an open Bible and a ready heart, willing to pray and wait upon the Lord. Paul must be relearning the scriptures he knew from being a Pharisee and seeing it in a new light, through the eyes of His Saviour. The revelations given to him were a testament to the weight of his calling. He talks much about prayer in his writings. He teaches about praying in the Spirit, about praying without ceasing, about the role of the Holy Spirit when we pray. He exemplified intercession and so much more about spending time with the Lord in much prayer. He was indeed a man of prayer who knew the power of the secret place!

John the beloved

"I John, who also am your brother, and companion in tribulation, and in the kingdom and patience of Jesus Christ, was in the isle that is called Patmos, for the Word of God, and for the testimony of Jesus Christ." (Revelation 1:9, KJV)

John was put in lockdown in the island of Patmos for a very great purpose: he was the man chosen to receive the revelation of Jesus Christ about the last days. His banishment to Patmos was according to Historians, a punishment for the crime of being a Christian and for prophesying which was viewed by the Romans as belonging to the practice of magic and astrology punishable by banishment according to Roman tradition at that time. It was a result of antichristian persecution under the Roman emperor Domitian. But this has a far greater purpose than what the authorities have thought.

John was taken away from the stress and chaos of the ongoing persecution of Christians during his time for God to reveal to Him what is about to happen in the coming last days. His lockdown was for a special purpose and indeed we saw how John entered this place with such fear and trembling! To be shown the vision of Jesus Christ and his throne with all the angels and splendour of heaven must have been overwhelming! At some point he fainted and had to be picked up by the angel to regain his strength. It must be an awesome experience to receive all these revelations which we are now reading and more so watching it being fulfilled every day in our lifetime!

Sometimes God may take us away for a while for a specific purpose. He might want us to rest a while. Jesus told his disciples to come away for a while and rest. He said in Mark 6:31 to His disciples after a terribly busy day of ministering;

"Come away with me by yourselves to a quiet place and rest a while." Here we can see the necessity of lockdowns, spiritual lockdowns to rest a while and to be refreshed by the Lord. He did this even to Elijah when he got depressed about Jezebel's threat to take his life. The Lord sent an angel to minister to him, refreshed him physically and then dealt with him spiritually to get him back to the ministry again. (I Kings 19:4-14)

He who dwell in the secret place of the most High shall abide under the shadow of the Almighty.

Psalms 91:1

13

Staying in the secret place

Abide in me and I will abide in you. Just as no branch can bear fruit of itself without abiding in the vine, neither can you bear fruit unless you abide in me.
John 15:4

Abiding in Jesus. This is the secret to staying in the secret place.

In John 15 we see Jesus talking about the necessity of abiding in Him. He likened us to a branch in which He is the vine and God the father is the gardener. He wisely taught us that only when the branch remains in the vine that it can bear fruit. He said no branch can bear fruit by itself, it must remain in the vine. In essence, neither you nor me can bear fruit unless we remain in Him.

The secret place is the place where we remain connected to the vine. It is where we find the constant flow of life from the living water and the place where we always have our daily bread, the living bread. Jesus said, we will never be thirsty again nor be hungry again. It is in the secret place that we find this outflow of life from our living Saviour. Our daily communion with Him keeps us abiding in the vine. That is what keeps us connected to Him, allowing the flow of His life to flow through our own life and therefore we will bear fruits. First, the fruits of the Holy Spirit, showing in our character. We are becoming like Christ in our attitude and behaviour. Galatians 5:222-23 says, "But the fruit of the Spirit is love, joy, peace, forbearance, kindness, goodness, faithfulness, gentleness and self-control. Against such things, there is no law." (NIV)

To abide means to dwell. To dwell means to live in Him. This seems profound but Jesus made it simple by explaining that abiding in Him is just like a branch staying connected to the vine. The branch will not have an outflow of life without being connected to its vine. Once cut off from the vine, the branch soon withers away and die. It then becomes good for nothing. It will be gathered and thrown into the fire. It cannot bear fruit by itself. It needs the life coming from the vine to bear its fruits. Looking closely at this analogy, the fruits produced do not really come from the branch but from the vine. It comes because of staying connected to the vine and therefore it was able to bear its fruits. Our life's calling to be conformed to the image of Christ is a lifelong process of sanctification. It can only be achieved through our abiding in Him. Staying in the secret place will allow us to continuously connect to our Saviour and abide in His love. Therefore, staying in the secret place is of paramount importance to our lives as a christian. If we stay in the presence of God, we learn to walk with Him each day. We are slowly becoming like Him in our character and this is the first fruit God expects to see from us. Out of these fruits of a godly life will come the power to witness and share the Gospel as people will see its reality from the lives of those who bring this Good News. In the book of Acts, we see this very clearly. On one occasion when Peter and John healed a paralytic man and they were brought in front of the leaders and elders to be questioned, they marvelled at how they answered them. "Now when they saw the boldness of Peter and John, and perceived that they were uneducated, common men, they were astonished.

And they recognised that they have been with Jesus. (Acts 4:13, ESV) People will notice if we are being in the presence of God. As Peter and John said, they cannot help but speak about what they have seen and heard. Being with Jesus every day and hearing from Him, seeing His holiness and goodness will make us into a natural evangelist! We will say along with the early apostles that we also cannot help it but speak about what we are seeing and hearing from our secret place! Knowing God is the key to being a fruitful Christian and staying in the secret place, abiding in Christ is the key to knowing God.

" The power to stay in the secret place lies in the
love that burns in our hearts for the One to whom
our soul gaze upon every time we meet out loving
Saviour in the secret place of prayer. "

I give them eternal
life, they shall never
perish; no one will
snatch them out of
My hands.
John 10:28

14

The temporary and the eternal

For this light momentary affliction is preparing for us an eternal weight of glory beyond all comparison, as we look not to the things that are seen but to the things that are unseen. For the things that are seen are temporary, but the things that are unseen are eternal.

2 Corinthians 4:17-18

We Christians must simplify our lives or lose untold treasures on earth and in eternity. Modern civilisation is so complex as to make the devotional life but impossible. The need for solitude and quietness was never greater than it is today.

A. W. Tozer

When Jesus told Martha, that what Mary have chosen will never be taken away from her, He is talking about the eternal value of Mary's choice. A wise decision when choosing between investing our time and money for things that will last for eternity or for things that will give us earthly gains. We always will have two options: invest in something temporary or invest in something that will give us eternal dividends. Investing in what truly matters in this life and into eternity is a choice we can make when spending our time, money, or resources. These are entrusted to us by the Lord and He expects us to be good stewards of these things. We want to hear a well done from Jesus at the end of our life's journey. We want Him to say to us; "Well done, good and faithful servant".

What will it take for us to become a wise investor? In a worldly sense, we are to choose which investment will give us a better return for our money. A good investment requires careful analysis and measured decision. Even in these earthly, temporary matters, we learn that investing into something with lasting value makes a good investment. What about in God's kingdom?

Let us explore a little bit about the concept of temporary and eternal in this life. Doing this will help us not only live a wise and joyfully contented life here on earth but also will help us prepare now for eternity.

Looking at things here on earth using heavenly perspective will help us make the right choices in this life. It is simplified by Paul when he divided the two into things that are seen and unseen. The things that are seen are temporary. The things that are unseen are eternal. Let us look closely into these two categories. What are the temporary things in life? First, this present life that we have is temporary. James 4:14 says "What is your life? You are a mist that appears for a little while and then vanishes." (NIV). Everything that we see right here in this life are all fleeting and will be here today and gone tomorrow. Money, houses, career, prestige, investments and all of life's pursuits and struggles will be gone with us when our life ended. It will be foolish to invest our everything into this temporary existence.

In contrast, let us look at the things that are unseen, for they are eternal. First, the soul of man is eternal. This is a very sobering truth. Mark 8:36-37 expressed this awesome truth;

"For what shall it profit a man, if he shall gain the whole world, and lose his own soul, or what shall a man give in exchange for his soul? (KJV) Jesus talked about a man here who wanted to buy a bigger barn to put all his harvest in. We read this in the parable of the rich fool; "And he told them this parable: "The ground of a certain rich man yielded an abundant harvest. He thought to himself, "What shall I do? I have no place to store my crops." Then he said, "This is what I'll do. I will tear down my barns and build bigger ones, and there I will store my surplus grain. And I will say to myself, "You have plenty of grain laid up for many years. Take life easy; eat, drink and be merry." But God said to him, "You fool! This very night your soul will be demanded from you. Then who will get what you have prepared for yourself? This is how it will be with whoever stores up things for themselves but is not rich toward God.""

Are we richer here on earth than we are in eternity? To be rich toward God is to choose to invest our earthly resources in things of eternal consequences and value. For example, helping the poor and needy with a longing to also see the same people know the life changing power of the Gospel. We can use our money and our time to reach out to the lost and show the love of God to a hurting generation. Every time we choose to give our resources for the advancement of the Kingdom of God, we are investing in eternity and we are choosing the eternal over the temporary. This is the best investment we can make here on earth.

Recognising that our life here on earth is only a temporary existence will help us to live with eternity in mind. It will help us make the right choices when it comes to spending our time and money or using our resources. We can convert earthly things into investments for eternity by carefully using our allotted time and money to advance the cause of Christ on this earth. By giving your hard earned money to help the poor, support a missionary, print bibles for the unreached and using your time to pray for mission works and evangelism and actually going yourself, you are being a good steward of all that the Lord has entrusted to you whilst living in this world.

Let us choose the eternal over the temporal while we still have the time to invest in what truly matters in this life. One day, we will all stand before the judgment seat of Christ (2 Corinthians 5:10); and only what is done for His name and for His kingdom will stand the test.

"I have found a pearl of great price. My purpose, my design. I know why I am here and why you created me... and for this ONE thing only, I will live."

15

Prayer of Commitment

Until one is committed, there is hesitancy, the chance to draw back. Always ineffectiveness.

-W.H. Murray, The Story of Everest

Lord, help me begin to begin!

- George Whitefield

Everything we have learned from this book will not matter unless we commit to seek the Lord and find our secret place. Commitment is the key to living and walking in the power of God's presence. Without commitment, we will not be able to even begin to find our secret place.

I encourage you to make a commitment to seek the face of God and know His presence. You can start by committing to set a time and choosing a place where you will meet with God every single day. Then you must begin. As George Whitfield once prayed; 'Help me begin to begin.'" You must do it and attend to the appointment you have committed yourself to do. Remember, it is an appointment with the most High God. It will be the most important appointment of your day, each day of your life. Nothing should supersede this no matter what happens to your daily routine. It must take priority as if life and death depend on it. For the life or death of your spiritual life truly depends on this ONE thing.

I want to share with you a prayer of commitment which I wrote many years ago when I learned about God's calling upon my life. From that moment onwards, I have made sure I pray this commitment periodically to remind myself about the pact I made with God and the promise I said to Him. This practice helps me never to retreat or give up no matter how difficult the road has become in my life's journey as a missionary and a servant of God.

A Prayer of Commitment

Knowing you Lord Jesus is finding a pearl of great price.
The excellence of knowing you cannot be compared to
anything on this earth. I count all things as lost in
comparison to knowing you. My own dreams and
ambitions, my own desires, accomplishments, and
rewards- these are nothing compared to knowing you.

So here I am Jesus... have all of me. I do not want to limit
what you can do on the earth by the areas I
allow you to use in my life. Use all of me. From my very
last breath and drop of my blood... my every
bone and flesh, every cell and tissue in my body, I give
for you to use. To reach out to those
unreached... to those who have never heard of your name.
For with all my strength and with all that I am, I will lead
these precious souls to you.

I have found a pearl of great price. My purpose, my
design. I know why I am here and why you created me...
and for this ONE thing only, I will live.

I will do more than what the devoted communist did. I
will surpass whatever they were able to

accomplish. For I am a Christian. I carry Christ in me. I am commissioned to bring Him to the whole world. My ambition, my one dream is to get the name of Christ honoured and worshiped by every

tongue and tribe and people to the ends of the earth.

I am willing to give all that I have for this cause. Even if it will cost me to give up all that I hold dear in this life. My career plays a little role if it hinders me. My family, even my very own self and my own ambitions, these are secondary compared to this mission.
I am willing to give all that I am even if it will mean death to my own body, for it is my body only that the enemy of Christianity can take away from me... and yet' it will be restored back to me on that Great day.

So, I have nothing to fear and I fear nothing. For the love of God for the lost humanity far exceeds all fear. Send me, Lord send me to those savages... to even the cannibals and the fiercest communists, for I delight to be used by you and my life to be an offering for the glory of your name.
Even if it means danger on every side, jungle or abandonment, prison or even death itself. If I am where you wanted me... I will not wish to be anywhere else.
I love you, Lord Jesus.

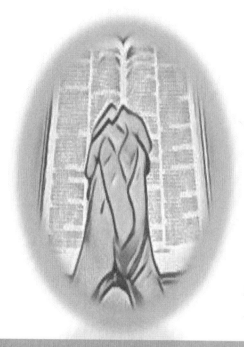

I pray that the Lord will help you and strengthen
you as you take the most important step of your
life; that is to put God first and to seek Him with
all your heart. May you find your secret place and
may you learn to dwell in it for the rest of your life.
There is no greater joy than this.

AN INVITATION

If you are reading this book but you are not sure if you have experienced an encounter with God which has awaken your soul to your great need of a Saviour, please do not let this opportunity pass you by.

The Bible says in Romans 6:23; "For all have sinned and fall short of the glory of God, there is no one that does good, no not one." There is no one who can stand guiltless before a holy God. We all deserved the judgment of God because of our sins. For the wages of sin is death but the gift of God is eternal life through Christ Jesus our Lord.

But God demonstrated His love for us, He showed mercy to each of us, He sent His only Son, Jesus Christ, to redeem us back to Himself by His own blood. For without the shedding of blood, there is no remission of sins. He came to set us free from the bondage of sin and death. An encounter with Christ enables us to see Calvary in a personal way. He promised forgiveness and freedom to those who would believe in Him. For whoever believed in Him shall not perish but have eternal life.

144

The moment you believed and received Christ as your personal Lord and Saviour, the Holy Spirit will come and dwell inside your heart. This is how you will know that the living God indwells you. The Spirit will testify inside your own spirit that you are a child of God.

A personal knowledge of the Saviour in our lives is indispensable to our relationship with God. A walk with God in the secret place each day is only possible once you have received Christ into your life. You will know of His forgiveness and guidance as you seek to do His will.

If you desire to know Christ in a personal way, simply pray and ask Him to come to your life and ask Him to open your eyes to see what He has done for you on Calvary.

You can pray this prayer.

Almighty God, I acknowledged that I am a sinner, I have sinned against you, I have chosen to do my own will. I admit and deserve your wrath and judgement. I asked for your mercy and forgiveness. I repent of my sins before you and believe in Jesus Christ, His death and resurrection. Thank you, Jesus, my Lord and Saviour for paying the ultimate price for my sins. I received you into my life. Be my Lord and Saviour from today and please help me to live a holy life for you. Amen.

References

Kane, S. (2018). The Hidden Benefits of Silence. Accessed 20 April 2020 through http://www.psychcentral.com/blog/thehidden-benefits—of-silence

Wurmbrand, R. (2018). Tortured for Christ: The Complete Story. the Voice of the Martyrs.United Kingdom: David C. Cook

Harrison, E.M. (1996-2020). *David Brainerd: Aflame for God.* Accessed 15 June 2020 through http://www.wholesomewords.org/missions/biobrainerd2.html

Reno, J.P. (2020). *Daniel Nash 1775-1831 - Prayer Warrior for Charles Finney.* Accessed 16 June 2020 through http://www.hopefaithprayer.com/prayer-warrior-charles-finney

Loizides, L. (2009). *Prayer and Passion in the Journals of George Whitefield.* Accessed 16 June 2020 through http://www.google.com/amp/s/lexloiz.wordpress.com/2009/08//18/ prayer-and-passion-in-the-journals-of-george-whitefield/am p

Cobb M. (2013). *John Wesley's Prayer Life.* Accessed 17 June 2020 through http://www.micahcobb.com/blog/john-wesleys-prayer-life

Green, J. & Green- Mcafee, L. (2018). *The Praying Example of Susanna Wesley.* Accessed 16 June 2020 through http://www.faithgateway.com/prayin g-example-susanna-wesley

Harrison, E.M. (1996-2020). *J. Hudson Taylor: God's Mighty Man of Prayer.* Accessed 17 June 2020 through http://www.wholesomewords.org/missions/biotaylor3.htm l

Torrey, R.A. (1996-2020). *Why God Used D.L. Moody.* Accessed 18 June 2020 through http://www.wholesomewords.org/biography/biomoody6.html

Swearingen, C & P. (2020). Beautiful Feet/ *Revival on the Island of Lewis: 1949-1952*. Accessed by 07 July 2020 through http://www.romans1015.com/lewis-revival

Peckham, C & M. (2004). Sounds from Heaven: The Revival on the Isle of Lewis, 1949-1952. Glasgow, United Kingdom: Christian Focus Publications

All scripture quotations are taken from the Bible Gateway Online Resource. Accessed through http://www.google.com/amp/s/www.biblegateway.com

Acknowledgement

I want to thank my parents for teaching me the most important lesson in life: To always do the right thing no matter what the cost. I also want to acknowledge my best friend and most loyal and faithful confidante, Rowena Balmeo. Her support and encouragement helped me to finally sit down and write this book. Above all, I want to thank Jesus Christ my Lord and Saviour. The lover of my soul, to whom I owe everything and for whom I live this life each day until I breathe my last. You are my pearl of great price, my treasure beyond compare. No one and nothing in this world is more worthy than you.

Marivic Quiazon

July 2020

About the Author

Marivic is the founding missionary of North Korea & Beyond Missions International. She travels extensively as an itinerant Bible teacher and works with native pastors around the world in reaching out to the most unreached people groups with the Gospel. She divides her time in doing overseas missions and working as a nurse in the United Kingdom. She also speaks in churches and conferences around the world. An anointed and gifted speaker, she brings the freshness of the Holy Spirit's presence whenever she is preaching or teaching. She enjoys painting and photography in her spare time and loves taking a long walk while listening to her favourite worship songs.

Printed in Great Britain
by Amazon